THE BRUCE DUBBIN MEMOIRS

THE BRUCE DUBBIN MEMOIRS

STORIES OF A POLICE OFFICER

ISBN: HARDCOVER 978-0-9880755-0-4

Printed in Canada

To Order Additional Copies of this book, contact:
www.brucedubbin.com
brucedubbin@gmail.com

This book is dedicated to all those who have died in the line of duty and to their families who hold them in their hearts.

I would also like to dedicate this book to the memory of my brother Harold William Dubbin, my editor, and my mentor. Bill I could not have done it without you.

~ Love, your brother Bruce ~

I would like to gratefully acknowledge all of my children who contributed money to the publishing of this manuscript and to Brad Steckel for contributing his time reading and editing. My oldest daughter Deanna Dubbin spent countless hours, typing and re-typing these chapters and facilitating the publishing of my book. For that, I am forever grateful.

Thanks go to Chief Constable Brian Sawyer, who gave me permission to gather information from files containing stories depicted in the book and thanks to Ruth Bragg, a Police employee who typed my manuscript several times on her own time.

And finally, thank you to my devoted wife Nina Dubbin. I will love you always! ~ Bruce

Contents

A Message to Our Dad

GERRY DUBBIN ~

Dear Dad ~ I clearly remember the first time I read this manuscript. For weeks on end, I saw you in front of that manual typewriter. I had no idea what you were creating. I had no idea at the time that it would become so profound for me. Your stories, your candor, and above all your honesty made so many things crystal clear for me. Having walked your path, I now understand the courage it took to reveal yourself and the pain you suffered being judged and misunderstood. In spite of it all, you forged on in a desperate attempt to survive it all. You once said to me that I would scale a mountain of glass to succeed and you were right. That was the beginning of my own recovery process.

You raised six of us, all over achievers. My best ever memories of us as adults, was seeing the smile on your face, sitting in the audience at one of our shows and hear you brag about all of us and our chosen careers to someone on the phone.

Not all of us survive this but you did Dad. Sharing your stories and helping me understand that dark passenger who rode with you for so long, trying to highjack your thoughts. I survived it too. I managed to rid myself of that dark passenger thanks to you sharing with me. One of my greatest joys now is doing what you did for me, sharing the dark stories with the young people in my life. As your oldest son, you taught me how to be a protector and I took over that role with our family when you were in the hospital. That behavior remains with me today. As kids, you embraced our friends, our relationships. You even invited one of my friends to live with us when he had nowhere to go. You were the coolest Dad ever, in the eyes of us all.

This book is your legacy. Your words and your honesty have been a profound influence on me, your family, generations to come, and now, the world. I can't think of a better gift. Congratulations Dad and Thank You. I Love you! Gerry

KEN DUBBIN ~

There was only one reason I was a five year old walking down Charleswood Drive in Calgary, wearing a tan trench coat in the middle of summer and using the concealed camera in my Secret Sam brief case to take photos of "evidence." I wanted to be just like my dad. That feeling stays with me to this day. Although I took a different path in terms of employment, I believe in the same things my dad does. My favourite memory is taking a ride along with my dad when I was seventeen years old. Dad was a detective in plain clothes and we got a call to a bank robbery at the Bank of Montreal on the Eighth Avenue mall. We arrived and I started looking in garbage cans in the area and found a trench coat. Dad treated it as evidence and I got to go to the police station and make a statement. It is highly unlikely it was evidence in the robbery, but I felt like a million dollars that day. I am and always will be my father's son.

I love you dad. ~ Ken

DEANNA DUBBIN ~

One of my earliest memories was trying to follow my Dad to work on my tricycle. I got lost and hence became a missing child that day, but was eventually found and taken home by my father's cohorts and fellow police officers. That was when I began to understand what my father did for a living. He took care of people. He helped people. He protected people with an unfaltering sense of who he was and what he was meant to do. I used to sit and watch Dad get ready for work. He was meticulous. Dad would foam up the brush, slather it on, then carefully, and slowly scrape it off with the razor, rinsing between each stroke. The entire process would be finished off by literally slapping on some Old Spice. The next step was polishing his shoes. He made his shoes shine like no one else. Finally the uniform - perfectly pressed. Dad's pride in being a Police Officer was in everything he did. He wanted to make a difference. He didn't care about the 'power of the badge'. He cared about helping people. He cared about seeing justice served.

As I read the pages of his book, everything that did not make sense to me so long ago, made sense to me now. Why did he have to be so over protective of all of us? I wanted to push the boundaries. I was a rebel who was always getting into trouble and getting grounded for staying out too late, not saying where I was going, hitch hiking, borrowing the car without asking and so on and so on. I was the oldest girl of six kids with two older brothers. I just wanted to be treated the same as them. I remember one day in 1971, my Dad came racing through the front doors of our house with his partner, asking if I was home. Something terrible had happened to a young woman not far from our house. I now understand the relentless fear that would gnaw away at him over time. He loved us so much! And he still does. Dad saw the 'ugly' side of people. He had to face it every day. So he made sure our lives were full of magic and fantasy that kept us young and innocent for as long as possible. He didn't want us to see what he saw. Ever!

Daddy you will always be the bravest man I know. Thank you for teaching me to trust my instincts.

Love ~ Deanna

MIKE DUBBIN ~

As I reflect upon the contents of Dad's book, I hearken back to observing Dad with wonder. There were days when I wondered as a child why Dad might be upset, frustrated, disappointed or in tears.

Today, as an adult, I see the world through my father's eyes. The destruction. The torment. The criminal justice system in chaos. Now I understand why my Father was protective of his six children to the extent that he was and still is to this day. Now I understand why my Father stood guard, literally, over his home, my Mom and all of us children. I don't understand the world. I do understand my Father and all he stands for.

You taught me to love. You taught me to serve and protect; my life partner, my children, my grandchildren and my home. My circle of influence, family, friends and associates know you through me and are deeply influenced by your presence as a hockey, baseball, football and life coach. Your influence and guidance will be with me all of my days.

Thank you Dad! I Love You! ~ Mike

DENNIS DUBBIN ~

"*To Serve And Protect*" The 'Mission Statement' of every policeman. In the dictionary the words serve and protect are defined as this; Serve; perform duties or services for (another person or an organization): Protect; keep safe from harm or injury. Father—In the dictionary the word father is defined as this; a man who gives care and protection to someone or something the oldest or most respected member of a society or other body.

Not only did Dad "serve and protect" his community, Dad served and protected his wife, his children and his friends. He was a father to six children, thirteen foster children and countless "strays". Dad you performed your duties as a policeman and a father not only as it is defined in a book, but as it is defined in life. You kept us all safe from harm or injury and you gave us all the care and protection we could ask for! You also gave me the greatest gift any father could give a son, you believed in me.

"*He's a man of great dignity, honor and strength. His merits are noble, and of admirable length. He's far greater than all other men that I know. He's my Dad, he's my mentor, my friend and hero*". Debbie Hinton Young.

DENISE DUBBIN ~

As a child, I was somewhat sheltered by my older siblings, therefore I did not truly understand the sacrifices my Dad made, not only for his family, but for the safety of the public. I knew that his work as a Police Officer often caused him much stress, but it was not until later in life that I truly realized the depth of his commitment.

When Dad joined the force he took an oath "To Serve and to Protect". I am so proud to say that he did just that, not only through his work but his family as well. I can always count on my Dad for his love, caring, protection, and mostly his support.

Thank you Dad for being my safe place. Love ~ Denise

INTRODUCTION

The Good Times

'Prison reforms are generally molded to assist those willing to be assisted. Little is done to discourage those who have violent tendencies or who are repeat offenders.'

Mandatory supervision, the most controversial of the "early" programs, was legislated in 1970 to act as a "watchdog" over known violent parolees.

A prisoner who escaped four times, murdered a fellow prisoner in 1971, and stabbed another in 1977, was released on mandatory supervision then arrested again for escaping lawful custody and being in possession of a gun.

Since his incarceration in 1966, the killer had "earned" four-and-a-half years off for "good behavior".

Prior to 1970, prisoners described as "dangerous" were released back into the community with no form of supervision. This was made possible under the provisions of the "Penitentiary Act". All prisoners were granted "statutory" remission amounting to one quarter of their sentence, along with "earned" remission at the rate of three days a month. The inmates knew this as "good time". Prisoners could only earn or be granted remission up to one third of their sentence. Remission is time deducted from a sentence and does not include parole. Once released on remission their sentence was deemed to be over.

Statutory remission was automatic. Earned remission was only to be granted to those prisoners who applied themselves industriously to the programs of the institute.

However, during an interview in The Calgary Herald in 1982, Jim Phelps, Corrections Canada Deputy Commissioner, stated that prisoners with records of severe prison misconduct almost, always "earned" some time off for good behavior.

"As long as a prisoner was getting up in the morning and going to work and not breaking institutional rules he would earn all of his remission," Phelps said.

Parole, a supervised program could be granted to an inmate who had served as little as one third of their sentence.

Often inmates with known violent histories who did not want to be supervised would refuse parole, opting to remain in prison until "full remission" or two thirds of their sentence.

With the introduction of "Mandatory supervision", all prisoners leaving a federal institute on "remission" were forced to take supervision.

In 1973, the Canadian Association of Chiefs of Police (CACP) applauded the mandatory supervision introduction as a further safeguard to society. The association believed that supervised criminals would be less likely to commit violent crimes.

Four years later, the CACP supported a move to have mandatory supervision and automatic remission abolished. They had reason for concern.

During a four year period from 1975 to 1979 offenders on mandatory supervision committed the following crimes: 31 Murders, 21 Cases of Manslaughter (a lesser degree of murder), 11 attempted murders, 25 rapes, 23 sexual assaults, 15 kidnappings, 394 robberies. 2,598 persons were revoked from mandatory supervision during this period.

The revocations then created a new problem known as the "revolving door syndrome". Prisoners who still had "earned" and "statutory" remissions on their record at re-entry were re-credited with this "good time" and were often released again within a few months.

Mass murderer Clifford Olson convicted of killing eleven children in British Columbia was one of those 2,598 persons revoked from mandatory supervision and released again.

Olson, who spent 21 of 24 years in prison or on parole between 1957 and his arrest for the murders in 1981, was released on mandatory supervision at least three times.

With previous convictions for armed robbery, break and enter, escaping lawful custody, parole violation, fraud, and possession of stolen property, Clifford Olson was sentenced to six and a half years in 1974 on forgery, theft and false pretence charges, (writing bad cheques).

Released on mandatory supervision in 1977 he was re-arrested two months later for fraud. Released again in January of 1978, he was arrested again in September 1978 for possession of housebreaking instruments. Fifteen months later in January 1980, he was released again on mandatory supervision, and recommitted five months later for impaired driving.

However, the wheels of justice continued to grind and Olson was released again on mandatory supervision in 1981. During the time he was released and arrested for the child murders, Olson was charged with several sexual offences, some of which were "stayed" (not proceeded with) or were still before the courts. However, Olson had completed his mandatory supervision before being arrested for the murders.

Records from the National Parole Service (NPS) community assessment papers revealed that Olson, while on mandatory supervision, had traveled to Calgary and Edmonton without permission. H.M. Wytinck, Edmonton National Parole Service assistant district director, penciled this admonition at the bottom of Olson's assessment paper.

"Being out of the area without permission is a breach of M.S. (Mandatory Supervision). Should be suspended."

The parole board ignored the advice that Olson should be returned to jail. Olson was also wanted in Nova Scotia on a charge of molesting a young girl in 1978. Statutory remission is no longer credited to inmates, (automatic time off sentence) however they can earn up to 15 days a month for "good behavior".

Various forms of parole may be granted to inmates of provincial and federal prisons. The jurisdiction of granting such parole lies with the parole board or the governing provincial body.

"Temporary Absence" may be granted to an inmate for humanitarian or rehabilitation purposes. Allan Bloome (I'd Bet My Life) was granted such a pass.

The parole board may grant "Day Parole" to an inmate after the board has determined that such parole will not constitute an undue risk to society. Kristen Kjeldsen (By Reason of Insanity) was on day parole from a British Columbia Institute when he fled to Calgary, raped, and attempted to murder a young girl.

"Full Parole" may be granted to any prisoner who has served one third of their prescribed sentence, but they must report to parole officials until expiry of sentence.

'Serving' prisoners in provincial institutes are released after serving two thirds of a sentence and do not have to report on parole.

The parole system that was designed to assist men and women back into our society after prison confinement appears to have lost its original intent.

Prison reforms are generally molded to assist those willing to be assisted. Little is done to discourage those who have violent tendencies or who are repeat offenders.

An inmate who was serving a three-year sentence was denied parole. After serving 24 months, he was released on mandatory supervision by virtue of "earned remission" or "good time". While on mandatory supervision he was arrested for another offence and suspended by the parole board. On sentencing for the most recent offence, the man received a 15-month sentence to run concurrent with the sentence he was on mandatory supervision for. On return to the penitentiary, he was re-credited with his previously earned 12 months remission. After serving only two months of his new sentence, the man 'earned' an additional one-month "good time".

With a total of 12 months remission to his credit, he was released again on mandatory supervision after serving only two months of the 15 months.

Roger Niesman, a young Southern Alberta father was sentenced to eleven months for assaulting a man convicted of molesting his six-year-old daughter. The molester was convicted but remained free on bail almost two years after the incident pending an appeal.

Niesman released after serving five months of his eleven-month sentence was confined to his hometown by probation. The suspect child molester moved to Ontario awaiting his appeal.

In 1983, Maurice Michel, a convict serving nine years for armed robbery, was charged with murdering a prison guard. The guard, Leandre Leblanc was on his last shift before retirement when Michel and two other prisoners dragged him screaming from his office at the penitentiary. A hushed courtroom listened as Jean-Paul Levesque, a serving prisoner of the same penitentiary, described the last moments of the elderly guard. "He was looking at pictures of his family and crying as the convicts burst in on him", Levesque said.

Found guilty of first-degree murder, Michel was sentenced to life with no parole for 25 years. However, a proviso in the Criminal Code allows killers such as Michel to ask for a review of parole eligibility time, after serving only 15 years.

Incidents like these are what the Canadian public must live with. Since the abolishment of capital punishment and the insertion of section 672 (1) into the code (reduction of parole eligibility time), Canadians can no longer be assured that men like Michel's will not be free to murder again.

The justice system, in dealing with men like Clifford Olson and Maurice Michel, appears to be thumbing its nose at the Canadian public. For all the government rhetoric, little is being done to assure the public that their safety is of prime concern.

The more prevalent a crime becomes, the more likely the courts are to accept it as near normal behavior.

In the early fifties, a Calgary man was sentenced to 25 years for bank robbery. Another man was sentenced to 25 years and to be whipped for raping a 14-year-old girl. Similar crimes today would result in sentences of less than five years.

During the eighties two men were convicted of manslaughter for killing a member of a motorcycle gang. Evidence at the trial revealed the two accused had stalked the victim as he rode his motorcycle along a Calgary street. Pulling along side the victim, they literally "blew" him from his bike with a shotgun blast. The killers received four-year sentences.

In January of 1986, Yves "The Mad Bumper" Trudeau, an ex-member of the "Hells Angels" motorcycle club, received a life sentence after pleading guilty to 43 counts of manslaughter. Trudeau admitted to police that he had personally murdered 43 victims in a series of gangland style killings and probably had a hand in at least 40 more. With a life sentence imposed, other than a minimum punishment commonly referred to as "life maximum", Trudeau will be eligible for parole seven years from the time he was arrested. He will also be eligible for day parole five years from the date of sentencing and eligible for temporary absence four years from full parole eligibility of 1993.

Trudeau negotiated his short sentence with the crown prosecutor and the Quebec Government after agreeing to testify against other gang members. Described by his peers as a man who killed at will, Trudeau has also been guaranteed a $40,000.00 cash settlement on his release from prison.

The Quebec Government has agreed to pay Trudeau $10,000.00 dollars of taxpayer's money for fours years plus $12,000.00 during his incarceration for such incidentals as cigarettes. Many honest Canadians will not make as much over the next years. Once released Trudeau and his family will be given new identities and relocated.

Section 215. (1) of the Criminal Code describes manslaughter as "Culpable Homicide" that otherwise would be murder may be reduced to manslaughter if the person who committed it did so in the heat of passion caused by sudden provocation.

Section 214. (2) of the Criminal Code describes murder, as "Murder is first degree murder when it is planned and deliberate". Canadians could question how a judge in good conscience could accept a plea of Manslaughter 43 times.

THE YOUNG OFFENDERS ACT

The "coddling" of such criminals is not new to our justice system, however in 1984 it took on a new dimension.

In a continuation of what can best be described as "ill-fated" legislation, our parliamentarians brought into force the "Young Offenders Act." The act, designed to deal with persons between the ages of 12 and 17 years old, came into force in 1984 replacing the "Juvenile Delinquency Act" of 1908. The act standardized what had been an unbalanced age factor. Previously, ages for juveniles had been left up to the provinces. Alberta at one time classified juvenile girls as those under 18 and boys under 16 years old.

The act standardized the age across Canada, but with it came problems. Offenders between the age of 16 and 18 years old previously dealt with as adults, once again became "juveniles" for the purpose of the act. This means that some young offenders had been through the system as adults and are criminally wise in their ways.

During the latter part of 1985 and the first months of 1986, ten young offenders escaped from the Bow River Correctional Center near Calgary. Because they are protected under the act, their names and pictures could not be published. Calgarians were left at the mercy of an act designed to protect only the guilty with no concern for the public.

Prior to these escapes, near riot conditions had existed at the center. At least one guard was injured during a disturbance. Reports had been leaking from the center for weeks that violence within the detention area was frequent.

In two separate incidents during February of 1986, Calgary Police were called to Young Offenders Court to quell disturbances. Reports from police indicate the youths were unhappy with holding facilities.

The act, apparently designed to protect young offenders from criminal association, is working in reverse. Children as young as 12 years old are now being detained in holding facilities with young offenders who have previous "adult" criminal records.

Reports from the center indicated that older inmates were brutalizing the 12 and 13 year olds. As one senior police officer stated, "That's going to happen when you put kids in with a bunch of punks".

Children under the age of 12 years who cannot be charged with a criminal offence have already surfaced to take advantage of the act.

An 11 year old in Toronto suspected of robberies, assaults and thefts laughed at police when stopped in stolen car. After setting a series of fires, the last one causing $50,000.00 damage, two eleven year olds in Calgary were caught but cannot be charged. Section 1(1) of the act describes a "child" as being under the age of 12 years old. Section 5 states that no person shall be found guilty of an offence under the act while he was a child.

The act does not properly address the more dangerous young offender by limiting sentences to a maximum of three years. This has Superintendent Ron Tarrant of the Calgary Police Service worried.

A 14-year-old Toronto boy charged with murdering a family of three, including a seven-year-old girl was sentenced to three years; the maximum under the act. At the trial, the crown chose not to have the youth transferred to adult court. If this had been done, the youth could have been sentenced to a longer term.

During the trial, two psychiatrists testified that the youth suffered a "disease of the mind." However, the judge refused to accept a joint submission by the crown and defense that the youth was insane at the time of the shooting. In making his ruling, the judge would not accept the fact that the youth could not appreciate the quality and nature of the act. Both elements are required under the code to establish insanity.

In an interview after the trial, Ontario Attorney General Ian Scott suggested the boy would no longer be a danger to the public because a psychiatrist will examine him when his case comes up for review.

Kristen Kjeldsen (By Reason of Insanity) was declared "no longer a danger to the public" when he was released and murdered Calgary taxi Driver, Glenda Ferster. Judge C.R. Ball who presided over the case said in a later interview, he "was not unmindful of the concerns of the public".

However, he said the blame for sentencing lies not with him or the Young Offenders Act, but with the crown's decision not to have the case transferred to adult court in the first place.

Judge Ball's comments seemingly did not agree with comments made by a Vancouver Supreme Court Judge several months later.

Mr. Justice Ken Meredith of Vancouver ruled that a teenager charged with murdering an eleven year old would not be tried in adult court. Justice Meredith had reversed a youth court decision that had found the teenager fit to stand trial in adult court.

Justice Meredith ruled that a stiff prison term would not benefit society and would likely harm the accused if he were found guilty.

Decisions such as these leave the community wondering about a judge apparently conversant in the matters of young offenders, overruled by a Justice sitting in a higher court. Must we assume that the lower court judge was not presented with all the facts in rendering his decision, or must we assume that the higher courts decision was based solely on defense arguments?

Justice Minister John Crosbie's analogy did not apparently agree with either Judge Ball or Justice Meredith when he said, "the Young Offenders Act does not properly deal with persons charged with serious offences."

The tragedy of such legislation leaves the victim's family distraught and angry. Unable to lash out at the courts they are left feeling that the justice system does little to punish those persons charged with violent crimes.

While Judges can openly criticize witnesses, responses by prosecutors and defense lawyers are done so at their own peril.

"Contempt", a section of the code, protects Judges from criticism.

To call a Judge incompetent or to suggest that a presiding Judge was "biased" or not capable of sitting on the bench can bring charges of contempt. Newspapers, newscasters, lawyers, and Policemen have been cited for written or spoken words.

The legal system often leaves the victims of crime frustrated with court procedures that continually delay trials. These frustrations have been depicted many times on television and movies. "And Justice for All" was one such movie that depicted the facilities of the system. "Rage", a television movie depicted how a known killer could be freed when his "rights" were violated.

Over two hundred years ago, Jonathan Swift, a famous English author, said that "Laws are like cobwebs which catch small flies, but let wasps and hornets go free".

Not much has changed since Jonathan Swift uttered those words.

CHAPTER ONE

By Judge Alone

"You are an extremely dangerous man to be at large....
you are free to go."

It was his dark eyes glaring at the top of my bowed head that somehow announced the stranger's presence. I'd been completing a report as I stood at the front counter of police headquarters on this sweltering night in July.

I raised my head and looked into the face of a man in his early twenties. He stood just inside the doors about 20 feet away as though he were afraid to approach me. I smiled to help ease his uncertainty. "Can I help you?"

It was Stampede week in Calgary with many tourists coming to our city, but this man didn't look like a tourist. He wore a light shirt and khaki colored pants. His shoes were dirty and scuffed and his hair unkempt. I repeated, "Can I help you?" He cautiously approached.

"I'm looking for my brother," he said desperately. His eyes darted from side to side as he shuffled nervously from foot to foot.

"What's your brother's name?" I asked.

"Robertson. Daryl Robertson."

"Don't you know his address?"

His eyes shifting downwards while replying "no".

I leaned forward on the counter and asked him his name.

"Denis."

"Denis Robertson?" I questioned wanting assurance both brothers carry the same last name.

"Yes" he replied.

"Where are you from Denis?"

"Toronto" he replied. "Toronto? What does your brother do?"

"I don't know. He just came here a couple of weeks ago."

"How long have you been looking for him?" I asked.

"I just got to Calgary last night. I couldn't find my brother." His voice trailed off as his eyes began darting back and forth once again and then suddenly he began to shake.

"Are you alright?" I asked.

"I'm wanted in Calgary for housebreaking" he blurted. Sensing that he might have second thoughts about turning himself in, I lept over the counter and stood beside him to prevent a hasty exit.

"Where did you break into a house?" I asked.

"Northwest" he replied.

"Northwest? Have you been here before?"

"I used to live in Calgary before I moved to Toronto with my brother".

"What the hell did you break into a house for?" I asked.

"I couldn't find my brother", he repeated, "I had nowhere to go."

"What did you steal from the house?"

"Just a few bucks and some food. I broke a mirror", he continued.

"Why did you do that?"

"I don't know. I guess I was just mad."

I stood for a moment looking at him. Something was wrong. Why would he come all the way to Calgary, break into a house then come to headquarters and turn himself in. It didn't make sense to me.

"Do you have some identification?"

He pulled out an old wallet and removed a tattered and torn driver's license. I studied it and sure enough, he was who he said he was. It read, "Denis Henry Robertson, Toronto."

"Okay. Come on. At least you'll have a place to sleep tonight and something to eat."

We proceeded into the office where I asked a constable to watch him while I went to pull the report on Robertson's case. Mr. Al Weitz, a bachelor on 21st Avenue Northwest had reported his house broken into on the night of July 7th, which was the previous night. It was reported the culprit threw a china figurine at a mirror destroying both. I took the report over to Robertson and asked if this was the house he broke into.

"Yes." he replied. "There's where it says the mirror was broken." He pointed his finger at the report.

"You will be charged with housebreaking," I explained as I lead him toward the elevator. "I'll book you now. Someone will probably come up and speak with you again. A team of detectives will see you before your court date."

Constable Syl Demers accompanied me to the charge office where I booked Robertson. "Any chance of getting this man some dinner?" I asked one of the booking constables. "I'll go look", he replied. Several minutes later the Constable returned with a plate of food and a coffee that Robertson quickly devoured while waiting to be booked. It looked like he hadn't eaten in a week. As I left the booking office I told him, "I'll see that someone comes up and talks to you later."

I returned to the front counter and put in my report on Robertson's arrest. With the report in hand, I went over to the detective office where Bob Pittman, Sergeant of Detectives was on duty. As I explained what happened, I kept feeling there was more to this story.

"There's something wrong here", I said to Sergeant Pittman. "I think he's got more on his mind than just finding his brother."

The sergeant's response was nonchalant as he mentioned he would have someone go talk to him. Several hours later, Detectives

Boyd Davidson and Dick Houger were sent to Robertson's cell to interview him. Davidson was a huge man at 6'2" and over 300 lbs with a neck that measured 22 inches in diameter. He was also a tenacious investigator. The two detectives questioned Robertson on his activities and how he got to Calgary. Why was he here? What did he do in Toronto?

Had he ever been in trouble with the police? Robertson changed his story several times, stating that he arrived in Calgary June 27th, not July 7th as he first mentioned. Why had he given himself up? As Detective Davidson studied Robertson during the questioning, he also felt that his story didn't add up. Something didn't fit. Robertson had more to worry about than a housebreaking. But what was it? Davidson excused himself and left the interview room. He returned to the detective office where he removed a poster from bulletin board. He studied the poster for several minutes. It was a composite drawing of a man wanted in Toronto for the murder of a male by the name of Gabriel Brunet. The murder occurred in a Toronto high-rise apartment on June 25th, 1967.

Detective Davidson returned to the interview room with the poster in hand. He sat across the table where he studied the drawing and then Robertson. Robertson began moving uneasily in his chair glancing nervously around the room. Suddenly Robertson began to shake uncontrollably as he dropped his head in his hands then jerked up out of his chair. His eyes were fixed in space as though looking at someone that wasn't there.

"I couldn't stand his screaming!" he yelled. "I had to do it! He wouldn't leave me alone. He wouldn't let me sleep. I was so tired. I had to do it!" Houger and Davidson sat silently for several minutes.

"What did you have to do?" Davidson asked.

"I had to come to Calgary", responded Robertson.

"Why did you come to Calgary?"

"I had to find my brother."

"Why did you break into the house and break the mirror?"

"I couldn't find my brother. I stole some money and some food."

Davidson and Houger continued to question Robertson on his activities in Toronto. During the questioning Detective Davidson was called to the phone. Robertson put his head in his hands again babbling incoherently.

Suddenly he yelled, "Oh God, how he screamed!" then sat bolt upright in his chair as though he was startled. He looked at Detective Houger. "What did I say?" he asked.

Detective Davidson returned to the interview room and spoke with Detective Houger. On being advised of Robertson's statement, Davidson questioned Robertson further. Robertson admitted that he knew Gabriel and had been at his apartment several times.

"Gabriel was a queer", Robertson said. "He never had any money".

"Where did you meet him?" Houger asked.

"At one of the downtown bars. He's a hairdresser. I was drinking there and he kept pulling at my arm. He wanted me to go back to his apartment to engage in a homosexual act. I didn't want to go with him. I knew he had no money but he kept pulling at my arm! I finally went up to his apartment and we had sex. I wanted to go to sleep so I went to bed. Gabriel came into the bedroom and wanted me to commit another homosexual act with him but I wanted to go to sleep."

Robertson stared into space, his eyes fixed on the wall. He appeared to be in a daze as he rambled on. "He kept pulling at me. I told him to leave me alone! I kept getting madder and madder!" Robertson went into a frenzy waving his arms and yelling.

"I told the fucking little queer to leave me alone! He kept pulling at me. I jumped out of bed, and ran to the kitchen and grabbed a butcher knife. I went back into the bedroom and started stabbing him. Gabriel jumped up and tried to hit me. I threw him on the bed and kept stabbing at him. Oh God how he screamed! I kept stabbing and stabbing him until he fell by the bed."

Robertson looked at the two detectives. He appeared to be relieved. "I went through his pockets but he didn't have any money. I got dressed and left the apartment."

"What did you do with the knife?" Davidson asked. There was no reply.

Robertson was cautioned and charged with murder and was held for the Toronto Police. While being placed back into the cells Robertson turned and said, "Okay! I killed the fucking little queer, but you'll never prove it. There's no prints."

Davidson returned to the detective office and phoned Toronto advising them of Robertson's arrest. The same morning Houger and Davidson interviewed Robertson again. Robertson admitted he hung around gay bars and made his living hustling homosexuals. Denis Robertson was a male prostitute. After the interview, Davidson and Houger returned to the detective office to make notes of Robertson's statements.

Sergeant Evans of the Toronto homicide division phoned to advise Davidson that he and Detective Dodson would be arriving in Calgary on July 10th to interview Robertson. On the arrival of the two Toronto homicide detectives, Houger and Davidson learned the circumstances surrounding the murder.

The victim, Gabriel, was seen leaving a bar on June 25th, with a young man known as Denis, at approximately 10:00 p.m. At approximately 1:00 a.m. on June 26th, Rene Cote, Gabriel's roommate returned to the apartment to find Gabriel's lifeless body lying in the bedroom. He had been stabbed 57 times. A witness saw a man fitting Robertson's description, stop at a jewelry shop near the apartment and check the time. It was 12:50 a.m. June 26, 1967. Rene Cote stated during questioning that he knew a young man by the name of Denis but didn't know his last name. Detective Mark Dodson and Sergeant Jack Evans interviewed Robertson, and had obtained statements from him admitting to the murder. More information was obtained about Robertson's behavior following the murder and leading up to his arrest. Robertson admitted leaving Toronto the day after the murder, breaking into several businesses while hitch hiking to Calgary, and selling his watch in Sault Ste. Marie.

During Robertson's cross Canada hike, he engaged in oral sex with an older man who picked him up along the way. This encounter resulted in Robertson contracting syphilis. The two Toronto investigators questioned Robertson on his background. Robertson stated he was from Lethbridge, Alberta. His parents were separated. Robertson said he and his younger brother would lie in bed at night listening to their mother have sex with the men she brought home. He admitted to the investigators that he hated his mother. He also admitted he would kill anyone who came between him and his brother.

On July 12th, 1967, Sergeant Evans and Detective Mark Dodson escorted Robertson back to Toronto. On October 20th, a preliminary hearing was held in Toronto where Detectives Davidson, Houger, and I gave evidence. At the conclusion of the hearing, Robertson was ordered to stand trial. The trial date was set for November 27th. Robertson elected trial by judge and jury. Mr. Justice Moran would preside. The Crown then presented its case and the defense lawyer called Robertson to the stand. Because the trial was being held before a jury, we entered in a voire-dire (a trial within a trial). At that stage of the proceedings, the jury was excused. It would be up to the judge to determine if the jury could hear Robertson's statements. Robertson took the stand. The defense lawyer started his questioning.

"Did you know the victim Gabriel Brunet?"

"Yes sir I did", Robertson replied.

"Did you kill the victim Gabriel Brunet on the night of June 25th, 1967?"

"No sir I did not."

"Do you know who killed Gabriel Brunet?"

"No sir I do not." Robertson appeared very confident as the questioning went on. He stood erect and answered the questions without hesitation.

"Were you with the victim on the night he was murdered?"

"No sir I was not." Defense Counsel's questions were very straightforward. Robertson had answered as expected. The prosecutor then commenced his cross-examination.

"Mr. Robertson is it not true that you knew the victim?"

"Yes sir I did."

"Had you not engaged in sex with Mr. Brunet on other occasions?"

"No sir I did not." Though appearing confident in his simplistic answers, Robertson started moving uneasily in the witness box. He shuffled from foot to foot. His glances toward his lawyer revealed his uneasiness.

"Were you with Mr. Brunet on the night he was murdered?"

"No sir I was not."

"What!" snapped the Crown Counsel? "Are you telling this court you were not with Gabriel Brunet on the night he was viciously murdered?"

"No! I mean yes."

"What DO you mean Mr. Robertson?"

"I mean I wasn't with him." Robertson became visibly shaken with tears streaming down his face as he glanced at his lawyer. Crown Counsel continued.

"Witnesses have testified in this court you were seen leaving the bar with Mr. Brunet. Are they lying?" Counsel's voice was loud and demanding.

"I don't know." Robertson answered.

"Witnesses have testified you were seen near Mr. Brunet's apartment at 12:50 a.m. looking in a jewelry shop window. Are they lying?" he yelled.

"I don't know", Robertson replied crying uncontrollably. Detectives Davidson, Houger and I silently watched this pathetic figure in the witness box. Robertson's lawyer dropped his head and nervously rolled a pencil in his hand.

"Why did you go to Calgary shortly after the murder?"

"I was looking for my brother".

"Did you give Detectives Davidson and Houger a statement telling them you killed 'the fucking little queer'?" Robertson's sobs could be heard above the Crown's booming voice.

"No! No!" screamed Robertson.

"Did you give Toronto investigators a statement admitting you killed Gabriel Brunet?"

Robertson didn't answer. Judge Moran sat with his hands folded under his chin watching the accused.

"Did you not give Toronto Police officers these statements admitting you killed Gabriel Brunet?" the Crown yelled while waiving statements over his head. Robertson looked at his lawyers pleading and screaming,

"Please help me!"

I glanced at his lawyer who was rolling the pencil rapidly through his fingers. Houger and Davidson sat with their arms crossed as they watched Robertson.

"I have no further questions", Crown Counsel said confidently as he sat down throwing the statements on the table in front of him. Justice Moran looked at the defense lawyer.

"Do you have any more questions?"

"No sir."

"In that case we'll adjourn for lunch. You're excused", the judge said looking at Robertson who then stumbled from the box crying.

"I don't think he should've done that", I said as we left the courtroom. "Defense sure as hell won't put Robertson on the stand in front of the jury now!"

After lunch, Justice Moran spoke to the defense lawyer and Crown Counsel. "I am satisfied the statements used were obtained properly. I am satisfied there was no inducement on the part of the Calgary or Toronto officers. I am satisfied that Robertson gave the statements voluntarily without fear of threat or favor. The jury may hear the evidence."

The jury was called back into the courtroom and Justice Moran instructed them on their duties. Once again, Davidson, Houger and I gave our evidence, this time in front of the jury. After we were done, Detective Houger and I returned to Calgary to await the verdict. The trial continued for several more days.

A week after returning to Calgary, Detective Dick Houger came to the front counter where I was working. "You're not going to believe this", he said. He caught me off guard as I had been daydreaming at my desk.

"Believe what?" I asked.

"Robertson's hearing turned into a mistrial."

"What?" I exclaimed.

"One of the jurors got sick and had to be excused so they had to declare it a mistrial. We'll be going back to Toronto when they set a new date."

"I guess I can live with that" I responded. I kind of hoped Dick was pulling my leg knowing that flying was not one of my favorite pastimes.

The following week I was informed by Detective Houger that we would be returning to Toronto for the new trial that had been rescheduled for February 5th, 1968. The trial would be heard in front of a judge alone. "There will be no mistrials this time", Chief Justice Leif of the Ontario Supreme Court said as he addressed defense and Crown Counsel.

After I took the stand and was sworn in, Crown Counsel asked me to relate to the court the circumstances surrounding Robertson's arrest. I explained to the court that, after Robertson had confessed to housebreaking, I jumped over the counter to prevent him from escaping. Justice Leif looked at me and said, "You did what?"

"I jumped over the counter to prevent him from leaving," I repeated. Justice Leif leaned back in his chair, threw down his pencil and asked with a scowl, "Is that the way you arrest people in Calgary?"

"Not usually", I answered, "this was not a usual situation."

The Justice allowed me to continue. I explained how I had taken Robertson to the booking office and requested a meal for him.

"What did the meal consist of?" Justice Leif asked.

"Potatoes, corn, meat, bread, and coffee."

"What kind of meat?" he asked curtly.

"I don't remember", I said apologetically. Justice Leif shook his head again leaning back in his chair.

After finishing my evidence, I left the stand feeling very intimidated. Detective Houger gave his evidence, followed by Detective Davidson who was then questioned by defense Counsel.

"Detective Davidson how tall are you?" Counsel began.

"Just over 6'2."

"How much do you weigh?"

"About 300 lbs."

"What size collar do you wear?"

"22 inches", Davidson replied.

"When you were questioning the accused, you produced a composite drawing. Did you ever show that drawing to the accused?"

"No I didn't", he said.

"You told the court earlier that you had studied the composite for some time while holding it so the accused could not see it. Is that right?"

"Yes sir. That's right", said Davidson.

"How long did you study the composite while keeping it hidden from Robertson?"

"Four or five minutes", Davidson answered.

"Four or five minutes!" Counsel shot back. "Did anyone say anything to the accused at that time?"

"No sir."

"That will be all. You're excused."

Crown Counsel then called Detective Mark Dodson and Sergeant Jack Evans to testify they had interviewed and obtained statements from the accused Robertson. As the Crown completed it's evidence, Chief Justice Leif spoke to defense Counsel. "Do you wish to call defense witnesses?" Defense Counsel looked over at Robertson who was sitting in the prisoner's box with his head down.

"No sir." Counsel answered. "We won't be calling the accused."

Justice Leif adjourned court having heard all of the evidence. When court was resumed, the following was Chief Justice Leif's summation:

> "*Statements obtained by Constable Dubbin have no bearing on the case and are inadmissible. Statements taken by Detective Davidson & Houger were taken in a compulsive atmosphere and cannot be considered voluntary. Statements taken by Detective Dodson and Sergeant Jack Evans related back to the Calgary statements and are therefore inadmissible.*"

All statements, verbal or written were declared inadmissible. Chief Justice Leif asked Robertson to stand up. "You are an extremely dangerous man to be at large, however, I find you not guilty. You're free to go." Robertson turned and ran to his lawyer, throwing his arms around him.

"Thank you! Thank you", he cried.

Detectives Houger, Davidson, Sergeant Evans, Dodson, myself and other officers giving evidence left the court and returned to our hotel. As we sat discussing the trial, none of us expressed any surprise at the acquittal. Chief Justice Leif said, "There would be no mistrial." And indeed there was not.

During the spring of 1972, Calgary was plagued by a series of rapes. Two men in an Oldsmobile dragged their victims from the street into the car. The girls were then driven to secluded spots where they were forced to perform sexual acts on the two rapists. The girls were subjected to pain and degradation as the two culprits vented their sexual desires on the helpless victims.

One victim who was driving alone at night was forced from her car, taken outside the city, and raped repeatedly. Another was attacked in her hotel room and subjected to two hours of horror. Late one night, Constable Arnie Wilson was being driven home by Lorne Brooks, a police chauffeur. While on the way home, they heard a police broadcast of an abduction of a 26-year-old woman. A description of the Oldsmobile was circulated. Instead of going home, Wilson and Brooks decided to check some of the outlying gravel pits.

As they approached a side road, they observed a 1971 Olds parked with its lights off. Brooks and Wilson left the police vehicle and approached the car. Looking in, they observed a man in the back seat fighting with a naked girl. He had his hands over her mouth, pushing her head down into the seat. A second male was watching from the front seat. Brooks and Constable Wilson opened the door and lunged at the two men, dragging them from the car eventually subduing and handcuffing them, then calling for assistance.

At headquarters, the two men were identified as Allen Brian Selbst and the aforementioned Denis Henry Robertson. When questioned by Detectives John Pettifer and Bill Stark, Robertson relayed the following story.

As a child, he indecently assaulted three eight-year-old girls. At thirteen, he was sent to Ponoka mental hospital where he remained until he was seventeen years old. He made his way to Montreal and then Toronto where he committed a number of rapes; many occurring in laundry rooms of large apartment buildings. In every assault, Robertson choked all of his victims before raping them, claiming that all girls liked to be hurt. "They're all crazy just like my mother. She used to like being hurt by men before they had sex. That's my secret with women. I hurt them before we have sex. They like that. They're all like my mother. They like a little pain before having sex. Why do they want to lock me up for having fun? You don't have to be married to have fun."

Robertson also told Detective Pettifer that he "killed a queer in Toronto but was found not guilty." Allen Brian Selbst was sentenced to eight years concurrent on each charge of four rapes. Denis Henry Robertson was sentenced to fifteen years concurrent on each charge of rape.

In his summation at the previous Robertson murder trial, Chief Justice Leif had said, "You are an extremely dangerous man to be at large." He then added the words that contribute to much of our sometimes senseless justice system. "You are free to go."

CHAPTER TWO

To Kill Again

"Never before had a man been convicted of murder by the use of dental identification."

Wayne Clifford Boden was a handsome 24-year old with thick, ear-length hair, which was parted in the middle topping his oval face. Like his hair, his friendly eyes were dark. Although his 5'8" frame carried only 160 pounds, his sloping shoulders were evidence of his upper body strength. The ever-present pipe clenched between his teeth gave him a distinguished look and he could have passed for a successful Businessman. Boden often bragged that, "Someday I'll be a millionaire." But one thing stood in the way of Boden fulfilling his dream—he was a pathological killer. Boden was born in Hamilton, Ontario on October 20th, 1947. With his high level of intelligence and smooth speaking manner, girls were at his command. Unfortunately, they knew nothing of his fiendish personality that periodically dictated the actions of Boden—Wayne Boden. Romeo! Murderer!

While living in Montreal, Boden had separated from his wife and cohabitated with a young girl. The girl, Susan McFarlane and Boden lived as man and wife. They moved to Calgary in 1970. Besides his wife, Boden left behind a small son and a string of bodies. After settling in Calgary, Boden traveled to Banff where he met an attractive woman named Elizabeth Porteous. She was a schoolteacher at Bowness High School in Calgary. Elizabeth was from a small town just a few miles from where Boden was born. This gave Wayne an opportunity to talk about common interests and explore common ground. He asked Miss Porteous if he could see her again. Elizabeth was flattered. Although she was nine years his senior, she replied that he could. Before they parted, she gave Boden her phone number. Back in Calgary that evening, Boden phoned Elizabeth and asked her out. She accepted, giving Boden her address. By coincidence, she lived only one block from Boden. Later that night Boden and Miss Porteous sat in the quiet Carriage House lounge, sharing drinks. When Wayne took her home, he asked her if he could call her again. "Sure", she replied as they parted. On Monday, May 17th, 1971 Boden phoned Elizabeth Porteous again, asking her if she would like to go out for a drink.

"Okay", she replied, "What time?"

"I'll pick you up at your apartment at 8:00 o'clock", Boden replied.

Boden left his 7th Avenue Southwest apartment at 7:50 p.m., telling Susan his common-law wife, he was going back to the tire shop where he worked. Wayne Boden returned to his apartment at 12:30 a.m., May 18th.

As he climbed into bed beside his girlfriend, she noticed that he was breathing heavily and sweating profusely. When questioned by Susan, Boden stated that he had run up the stairs from the parkade. At 7:30 a.m. Boden left his apartment for work. Susan McFarlane left shortly after for her job at a local bank.

Diane Field and Elizabeth Porteous lived in the same apartment building. Because both taught at Bowness High School, Diane had arranged to get a ride to school with Elizabeth on Tuesday, May 18th. Diane was to meet Elizabeth in the apartment lobby at 7:45 a.m. Mrs. Field rang the buzzer to suite 2506 where Elizabeth lived. She received no response. Believing that Elizabeth had slept in, Diane Field waited.

When Elizabeth Porteous hadn't come downstairs by 8:00 a.m. Diane picked up the house phone and called Elizabeth's suite again. There was still no response. Mrs. Field waited in the lobby until 8:20 a.m. She tried once more to contact Elizabeth Porteous without success. She then made other arrangements and left the apartment building. Elizabeth Porteous didn't arrive at school that morning. At 10:00 a.m. Len Ross, the school Principal of Bowness High, became concerned. He was certain that Elizabeth would have called in had she been sick. Mr. Ross had his secretary, Mrs. Booth call the apartment. She received no answer. She then called the apartment caretaker, asking him to check suite 2506 to see if Miss Porteous was all right. Mrs. Booth said she'd call the manager again in fifteen minutes. At 10:30 a.m., Mrs. Booth called the apartment manager a second time. Mr. Morris Lutz, the manager, assured Mrs. Booth that he'd check the suite as soon as he could and call her back. At noon, Mr. Lutz knocked on Miss Porteous' door, but again there was no answer.

It wasn't until shortly after 3:00 o'clock that Morris Lutz and Bill Mosley, the apartment maintenance man, tried again to arouse Miss Porteous. When they received no answer to their knock, Mr. Lutz opened the door with his passkey. The two men entered. They called Elizabeth's name but still there was no response. As they entered the suite, the two men noticed a broken shoe lying in the hallway. The window drapes had been torn from the rod and were heaped on the floor. Unable to locate Miss Porteous in the living room, they moved toward the bedroom.

As they entered, they spotted the lifeless body of Elizabeth Porteous sprawled on the bedroom floor. Her clothes had been ripped from her body. Morris Lutz hurried from the apartment, returning to his office where he phoned the police. In response, Constable Rick Talbott and Constable Fife arrived at the suite. After viewing the body, Talbott phoned headquarters advising the homicide squad of the situation. At 4:04 p.m. Detective Ed Madsen and Bill Brink arrived at the scene. A check of the suite indicated that a violent struggle had taken place. The condition of Miss Porteous' clothes alone indicated that she had fought furiously. Her dress had been ripped down the front, exposing her breasts and torn brassiere. The brassier had been ripped down from her shoulder causing bruising. Her undergarments had been pulled down and draped over her left leg. The contents of her purse lay strewn on the kitchen table. Detective Madsen called headquarters, speaking with Detective Sergeant Ernie Reimer, head of the homicide and robbery detail, advising him of the discovery.

The coroner and the identification bureau were notified to attend. Within minutes Sergeant Reimer, Dr. Waddell the coroner and his assistant Dr. Marx arrived. Subsequently, Detective Sergeant Don Nelson, Detective Bill Crabbe and Detective John Dyck of the identification bureau arrived. Doctors Waddell and Marx made a cursory examination of the victim. At 4:50 p.m. May 18th, 1971, they officially pronounced Elizabeth Porteous dead. Marks on Miss Porteous' neck indicated that she had been strangled. Marks around her breast appeared to have been made by teeth. It appeared the victim had been bitten during the life and death struggle. In their roles as homicide officers, the investigators hadn't seen similar marks on any other victims they'd examined. Detectives Brink and Madsen seized a number of exhibits from various parts of the suite. Included in the exhibits were several red buttons torn from the victims dress during the struggle.

The identification section took pictures of the body and the suite before Dr. Waddell ordered the body removed to the General Hospital for further examination. Constable Fife accompanied the body for continuity, while Detectives Brink and Madsen attended the hospital to witness the autopsy. Dr. Reynolds, the chief pathologist, performed the post-mortem. While removing the victim's clothing, Dr. Reynolds found a cuff link caught in Miss Porteous' dress. The imprint of the cuff link was visibly etched against the shoulder of the victim. It had obviously fallen from the shirt of the killer. A red button torn from the victim's dress was found inside her underclothing. Dr. Reynolds concluded that Miss Porteous had been strangled. She had been raped shortly before or after her death. Marks on her neck and breasts were consistent with teeth impressions. The killer had viciously bitten his victim during the struggle. Detective Crabbe of the identification bureau took pictures of the victim, paying particular attention to these bite marks. Dr. Reynolds estimated from preliminary examination that the victim had died between the hours of 5:30 a.m. and 8:00 a.m. on the early morning of May 18th, 1971. He had to wait for laboratory reports to be more conclusive.

Dr. Reynolds concluded his autopsy at 12:30 a.m. on May 19th. Madsen and Brink returned to headquarters to submit their reports and ponder the strange murder. As homicide officers, violence was not new to them. But somehow, this one was different. The detectives didn't rest easy as they left the station knowing they'd be back at the mentally exhausting investigation early the next morning. On May 19th, the investigator commenced the tedious task of interviewing people, relentlessly attempting to trace Elizabeth's final hours.

Detectives Don MacNeil and Les Goetjen were assigned to the investigation with Madsen and Brink. All leads had to be checked out and all information carefully sifted. One of the first to be interviewed was Mrs. Diane Field. She had arranged to ride to school with Elizabeth on Tuesday May 18th.

"I went down to meet her at a quarter to eight" she told investigators. "When she didn't show up I buzzed her suite. After getting no answer, I used the house phone to call her. There was still no answer. I waited until about twenty after eight. When I still couldn't contact her I made other arrangements to get to school."

Another of Miss Porteous' friends interviewed was Miss Marie Gazdaric, who also lived in the same apartment building.

"I phoned Liz about ten after seven on Monday. She told me she was going out."

'He's 24 and a bit immature', Liz had said in describing her date. 'But he's from down east. We should have something in common.'" Elizabeth told Marie the man's name was Wayne and that she'd met him in a bar in Banff. Another of Miss Porteous' friends who lived in the same building recounted her conversation with Elizabeth on Sunday, May 16th.

"At that time Liz had mentioned meeting a fellow by the name of Wayne in a Banff bar." As Sergeant Reimer and Detective MacNeil continued their interviews with Elizabeth's friends, it appeared that 'Wayne' might be involved, or at least be able to assist in the investigation. Miss Eden Free confirmed that Liz had a date on Monday, May 17th.

"I spoke with Liz at 7:30 and she said 'I can't talk long.' 'I'm expecting Wayne over any minute.'" Meanwhile, Detectives Brink and Madsen had returned to Miss Porteous' suite. Several more red buttons were located. Nothing more of importance was found. The four investigators met with Sergeant Reimer going over the statement and evidence they had. While talking, the phone in the homicide office rang. Sergeant Reimer answered it.

"This is Mr. Ross from Bowness High School. One of my teachers came to me today with some information. I don't know if it will be of any help to you. On the night of Elizabeth's murder, Harry Robinson, one of my teachers, and his wife Ruth, were driving on McLeod Trail when they saw Elizabeth Porteous riding in a Mercedes with a young fellow. He was about 23 or 24 years old with dark hair and good looking." Mr. and Mrs. Robinson were sure they could recognize the car.

Sergeant Reimer advised the others what he'd just been told. He hurried to the stolen auto detail, speaking to Detective Ernie Lund to have him check for similar cars registered in the Calgary area. Minutes later Detective Sergeant Reimer found what he wanted. A 1960 Mercedes Benz, blue in color registered to Wayne Clifford Boden of 927—7th Avenue Southwest. Detectives Don MacNeil and Les Goetjen were dispatched to the address. The investigators learned that Boden lived in the apartment with his common law wife, Susan McFarlane and that he was employed with a tire company. Boden's common law wife was located at the bank and taken to headquarters for questioning. Detective Sergeant Cec Byers and Detective Eric Brookwell were assigned to stake out the apartment. While Detective Goetjen interviewed Boden's common law wife, Detective MacNeil proceeded to the tire shop where Boden worked. However, Boden was doing sales calls and wasn't expected back until 4:30 p.m. MacNeil returned to the apartment building and kept the adjoining parkade under surveillance. At 4:45 p.m. Boden drove into the parkade in his blue Mercedes. Detective MacNeil approached the car.

"Wayne Boden?" he asked producing his badge.

"Yes I'm Wayne Boden", the stocky good-looking man replied.

"I'd like to have a talk with you at headquarters Wayne. Would you mind coming down?"

"Not at all", came the pleasant reply. "I'll just lock my car." Boden locked his car and accompanied Detective MacNeil to the police cruiser.

"What's this all about?" Boden asked as they made their way to headquarters.

"We're investigating an incident that happened in an apartment house the other night. We believe you can help us", MacNeil replied.

"I'll help if I can", the confident Boden replied. On their arrival at headquarters, Detective MacNeil took Boden into the detective office, placing him into the custody of Detectives Madsen and Brink.

"Wayne", Madsen started, "we're investigating the death of Elizabeth Porteous on or about May 18th and I understand you might be able to help us. Do you know her?"

"I know a girl named Liz", Boden replied.

"Where does she live?"

"Just around the corner from where I do."

"Where's that?"

"Well I live in Pentland Place on 7th Avenue West and she lives in an apartment on 9th Street and 7th Avenue.

"Is that O'Neil Towers?"

"Yes."

"When was the last time you saw her?"

"Well, I saw her Monday night when I was out with her."

"Did you pick her up at her apartment?"

"Yes. I left my place around ten to eight. Because of the one way streets, I had to drive around several blocks before I could park in front of O'Neil Towers."

"What kind of car were you driving?" Detective Madsen asked, leaning back in his chair and crossing his legs.

"My '60 Blue Mercedes."

"Did you go into the suite?" Madsen asked casually.

"Yes. Liz let me in." Boden shuffled uneasily in his chair as Madsen fired questions at him. Detective Madsen asked Boden some questions about his wait in the suite while Elizabeth was getting ready. Madsen asked him if he touched anything while he was in the suite. Boden replied that he touched several things.

"Was the curtain rod lying on the living room floor?"

"No. I don't think so." Boden replied. Boden told the investigators that he and Liz had gone to the Carriage House on MacLeod Trail and had several drinks, returning to her suite around ten to twelve. Madsen then asked Boden if he went into the suite with Elizabeth when they returned to the apartment. Boden replied that Liz gave him the key and he unlocked the door. Once inside Boden suggested that Elizabeth had asked him to stay for a cup of coffee. He stated he had refused because they both had to get up early in the morning. "I kissed her goodnight and left," Boden added. Madsen interrupted Boden.

"You mean to tell me it was you who turned down an invitation to stay and have coffee with an attractive girl like Liz?"

"Well we both had to get up early!"

"Did you lose anything while you were in the suite that night?"

"Yes I did."

"What?"

"A cuff link. I lost it before Liz and I went out. We looked for it but couldn't find it."

"You lost a cuff link? Would you know it again if you saw it?"

"Yes."

Detective Brink left the room and returned with a tin containing the broken cuff link. He opened the can and Detective Madsen showed Boden the broken cuff link. "Is that your cuff link?" Madsen asked Boden.

"Yes that's it" Boden replied.

Are you positive that's your cuff link?" Madsen repeated.

"Yes I am. I've had them quite a long time!" Detective Madsen sat back in his chair giving Boden a lengthy gaze.

"Wayne," Madsen said leaning toward Boden, "you're sure it's yours; and I'm positive that the person who lost that cuff link is the one who killed Liz! Wayne you are going to be charged with the murder of Elizabeth Porteous on or about May 18th. Do you understand?" Madsen asked.

"Yes." Boden replied. "I knew I was going to be charged five minutes after I came in here!" Detective Madsen then read the official caution to Boden.

"Having heard the charge, regardless of what's been said, you are not obliged to say anything unless you wish to do so. But anything you do say may be taken down in evidence. Do you understand?"

"Yes."

Madsen questioned Boden on the cuff link again. "You say you're positive that's your cuff link?"

"Yes. I was wearing them that night and as we were leaving the suite, my cuff kept falling down over my hand. I saw the link was missing.

We looked for it but couldn't find it."

"Do you still have the mate?" Madsen inquired.

"No. After I left that night I realized I had lost the one so I took my other one and threw it down the garbage chute in our apartment building when I got home."

Madsen continued to interview Boden on the events of the night in question. Boden described the clothing he'd worn, where he met Elizabeth and that he'd taken her out once before. Boden was questioned about the last minutes in the suite before he left her. "Wayne," Madsen continued, "there's no doubt in my mind that Liz was dead when you left the apartment that night. What happened? Did she refuse your advances?"

"Nothing happened!" Boden snapped. "She was okay when I left."

"Did she lock the door after you left?" Madsen asked. Boden replied that he thought so, as he'd heard her putting the night chain on.

"Wayne did you have intercourse with Liz that night?" Boden insisted that he had not had intercourse with Elizabeth Porteous on the night she was murdered.

At 6:00 p.m. May 19th, Wayne Clifford Boden was charged with the murder of Elizabeth Ann Porteous. After booking Boden in police cells, Brink and Madsen left headquarters to search Boden's suite. While searching, Detective Brink located a red button in the garbage container in Boden's suite. It was similar to those torn from the victims dress. Detective Sergeant Reimer continued to investigate Boden's background.

Contacting Montreal City Police, Reimer spoke with Detective Sergeant Rajotte of the Montreal homicide division. Reimer explained the arrest and circumstances of the Calgary murder. Rajotte related some startling information on Boden's background. While Boden was living in Montreal, three girls were murdered. Those cases remained unsolved. What appeared to be bite marks were present on all three bodies. Boden knew at least two of the victims. Though Boden had been a prime suspect in two of them, Montreal police had been unable to make any definite connection. Reimer told Rajotte that he'd keep him informed of Calgary's investigation.

During Boden's second court appearance, Ruth and Harry Robinson, both teacher's identified Boden as the person seen with Elizabeth Porteous on the night of the murder. Mrs. Robinson also identified the Mercedes car as the one Boden had been driving at the time. The investigation of Boden continued. On May 21st at noon, Sergeant Reimer and Detective Goetjen spoke with Boden again. Police officers who re-interview suspects must make it perfectly clear to them what charge they are facing. This is case law established in the 1940's, when a female suspect charged with an offence of vagrancy was questioned on a homicide. She admitted the offence, but was found not guilty because the investigators had failed to tell her she'd be charged with the murder of her husband in the case of Regina vs. Dick. Detective Sergeant Reimer introduced himself and Detective Goetjen.

"Hi Wayne. I'm sure you already have been informed as to the charges you are facing and clearly understand that you are charged with the murder of Elizabeth Porteous."

"Yes. I appreciate that." Boden replied.

"And I expect you've been told that regardless of anything you may have said before, you are not obliged to say anything now unless you wish to and that anything you say may be given in evidence."

"Yes. I realize that."

During the initial stages of the interview, Boden told Sergeant Reimer that he met Elizabeth Porteous in a Banff bar. Boden shifted constantly in his chair, refusing to look at Sergeant Reimer. He drooped his head and stared at the floor. He bragged about the fact that he had had many female conquests, never going more than a week without sex. "Wayne have you ever been treated by a psychiatrist?"

"There's been no need to."

"Do you think a normal male would dine a girl then strangle her, bite her breasts and have intercourse with her?"

"I don't suppose so." Again, Boden shifted uneasily in his chair. Reimer continued questioning but changed to the Montreal incidents. "I understand that you were also interviewed by the Montreal City Police regarding similar cases in that city."

"Yes. They interviewed me and had a line up."

"Obviously you weren't identified?"

"No someone else was."

"Were you interviewed on more than one occasion?"

"No."

"Were you questioned with respect to more than one murder?"

"I was only questioned briefly."

"Did you know any of the girls that were murdered?"

"Yes. One girl was Sue's friend."

"What was her name?"

"Jean Way."

"Do you know the names of the other girls?"

"There was Shirley Audette and Marie Archambault."

"Do you know where they lived?"

"Well Shirley Audette lived in an apartment on Dorchester, next to the one I lived in."

"Did the police talk to you at the time her body was found?"

"No."

"You mean they never spoke to you?"

"No."

"Did you remain living in the apartment?"

"For a while."

"Wayne have you seen a lawyer yet?"

"No. But I intend to plead not guilty." Boden reiterated he was not insane.

"I feel great both mentally and physically," he stated.

Sergeant Reimer referred back to Elizabeth Porteous again. "You may not have meant to kill her. Something triggered you. Something set you off. Did she do or say anything which would have made you lose your self control?" Boden replied "No" and dropped his head.

Boden reflected no remorse at Elizabeth Porteous' death, but suggested that he felt sorry for her mother. "Wayne", Reimer continued, "you are an intelligent man and I'm sure you appreciate that my job is to seek the truth. Would you tell me what happened?"

"I don't know why. I guess maybe I need psychiatric help."

"Tell me about it Wayne."

"There's not much to tell. It seems so vague now."

"Do you remember biting her?" Boden does not answer but nods 'yes'.

"Do you remember how many times?"

"Well, I know I bit her breasts."

"Did you panic after you killed her?"

"No not really." Wayne Boden was displaying signs of a pathological killer. He showed no sign of remorse for his victim.

After confessing to the Porteous murder, Boden asked for his pipe. Detective Goetjen brings it to him. Sergeant Reimer then suggested to Boden that he knew that he had killed before. Once again, Boden dropped his head.

"Yes" he replied to Reimer's question.

"Did you murder the three girls we spoke of earlier?" Audette, Archambault and Jean Way?"

"Yes."

"Would you tell me about the first one?"

"Well, I was coming home to my apartment on Dorchester. She was sitting on the steps of the apartment next door. She asked me if I had change for a bill, as she wanted to make a phone call. I told her that she could use the phone in my apartment. She came up to my apartment and she made a call. Then when she was leaving, I don't know what happened. I just went after her."

"What did you do with her body?"

"I carried her out and put her between the apartments."

"Did you have intercourse with her?"

"Yes."

"And the police never questioned you?"

"No."

"How about the next girl? Which one was that?"

"That was Marie Archambault" Boden replied.

"Where did you meet her?"

"In a discotheque."

"Had you met her before?"

"Yes."

"Where did you murder her?"

"In her apartment."

"How about the third one?"

"Well I knew Jean from before and I had dated her."

"Did you have intercourse with her?"

"Yes. I took her to a discotheque and then to her apartment where it happened."

Sergeant Reimer then asked Boden if he wanted to tell Susan McFarlane what happened.

"I'd like to see her" Boden replied. Detectives Don MacNeil brought Susan McFarlane to headquarters. In the presence of Sergeant Reimer, Boden admitted to her that he had killed Elizabeth Porteous.

The investigators' job wasn't finished. They now had to build an airtight case against Boden. Statements alone cannot be relied upon in court. Often they are dismissed on a technicality. Sergeant Reimer returned to his office to ponder the conversation with Boden. Reimer had read several British publications on teeth marks and identification. He wondered about the possibility of identification in this case. Sergeant Reimer contacted Dr. Gordon Swann, a Calgary Orthodontist. After explaining the bite marks found on the Porteous girl, Reimer inquired about the possibilities of these marks being identified such as fingerprints. Dr. Swann was intrigued. He knew it had never been done in Canada but he felt it was certainly worth a try.

"Would the accused consent to giving teeth impressions?" Dr. Swann inquired.

Sergeant Reimer didn't know, but said he'd ask the accused. If he consented, they'd bring Boden over to Dr. Swann's office. Boden agreed. Sergeant Reimer, Detectives Madsen, MacNeil and Brink escorted the accused to Dr. Swann's office. Dr. Swann took impressions of Boden's teeth. Investigators then took Dr. Swann to the morgue where he viewed the body of Elizabeth Porteous.

Detectives took more photographs of the victim's wounds. They were later enlarged for Dr. Swann's study. As he sat in his office pondering the task in front of him, Dr. Swann decided that he needed more information on how best to make the comparisons. He then contacted Sergeant Reimer, requesting that he contact the Federal Bureau of Investigation (F.B.I.) to determine if they had any information on similar investigations. The reply from the office of J. Edgar Hoover, head of the FBI was disheartening. They weren't aware of any such comparisons being made in the United States. However, they were certain that several British publications had written on the technique.

Dr. Swann, through several police agencies, was able to obtain written material on the procedure and set about the task of studying methods in other countries.

During the early part of July 1971, Dr. Gordon Swann left Calgary for England. Armed with a letter from the Calgary Police Chief, he visited Scotland Yard and spoke with several investigators. Once again, the doctor was disappointed to learn that Scotland Yard, like the FBI, had no case to refer to. Members of the Yard suggested that he go to the forensic laboratory located in London, which was attached to Scotland Yard.

On his arrival at the laboratory, Dr. Swann was referred to Keith Simpson of Guys Hospital in London. Professor Simpson was the head of the forensic department of the hospital. Professor Simpson had pioneered the use of dental science in criminology in Britain. He had considerable experience with identification of bite marks and other areas of dental identification. Simpson introduced Doctor Swann to B.G. Sims at London Hospital. Sims was in the Forensic Medicine Department. He provided additional information and references for Doctor Swann to study. Dr. Swann further met with Dr. John Furness in Liverpool. Furness was a dentist and a home office lecturer in forensic dentistry and had been consulted in some forty cases of murder in which bite marks were involved. After spending several hours with each of the experts in their respective fields, Dr. Swann returned to Calgary with a great deal of study material.

Taking the models he had made of Boden's bite impressions, he studied all aspects of the investigation. Later he conferred with several specialists from Eastern Canada and Calgary, who assisted him in his work. In early November of 1971, Sergeant Reimer contacted Montreal City Police, speaking again with Sergeant Rajotte. It was decided that Rajotte and Sergeant Turcotte, investigators of the Montreal murders, should visit Calgary, bringing with them photos showing the bite marks on the three murdered girls.

It was then possible that Dr. Swann could make a comparison of Boden's impressions from the pictures.

The two Montreal investigators arrived in Calgary on November 10th. On November 11th, Sergeant Reimer, Rajotte and Turcotte attended Dr. Swann's office. Dr. Swann was shown the pictures of the three murdered Montreal girls Shirley Audette, Jean Way, and Marielle Archambault. After examining the pictures, Dr. Swann concluded there were no identifiable marks on Jean Way. Bite marks on the body of Shirley Audette were evident. Unfortunately, the pictures had been taken after the autopsy, thus distorting the marks. Marks on the body of Marielle Archambault showed clearly in the picture. Dr. Swann offered the opinion that the marks were similar to those found on the body of Elizabeth Porteous. They appeared to have been made by the same person who inflicted the marks on Elizabeth Porteous. An analysis of these marks, utilizing the photographs of the study model and the wax bite impressions previously taken from Boden was made.

During the early part of February 1972, Dr. Swann did a preliminary analysis by utilizing enlargements of the photographs of Marielle Archambault, together with enlargements of the photographs made of the study model and the wax bite impressions of the suspect Boden. This resulted in a tentative identification of Wayne Boden as the person responsible for the bite marks found on the body of Marielle Archambault. Boden's trial was scheduled for February 15th, 1972. As a result, Dr. Swann was unable to confront Boden on his findings, for fear of interfering with the Crown's case on the Porteous murder. The three-day trial was held in front of Chief Justice Milvain of the Supreme Court of Alberta in Calgary. Prominent Calgary lawyer Mary Hetherington who was an ex-prosecutor herself defended Boden. Mr. Paul Chrumka handled the Crown's case.

Dr. Swann was sworn in, introducing the study models of the impressions made of Boden's teeth. He explained his introduction of an articulator, which was a machine, used to simulate movement of the jaws. The teeth are articulated in a functional bite relationship, showing all the characteristics of the teeth bite. Dr. Swann then explained to the court the formalities of how the models worked. At this point the Crown then attempted to have Dr. Swann recognized as an expert witness. Ms. Hetherington challenged the Crown's move, suggesting that though Dr. Swann was an expert in orthodontics, he was not necessarily an expert in dental identification. After hearing arguments from both defense and Crown counsel, Chief Justice Milvain ruled in favor of the Crown. After explaining his reasoning, Justice Milvain concluded, "I find that he (Dr. Swann) is competent in the field to give evidence that is to be given. The doctor is accepted as an expert in his field."

Dr. Swann continued his evidence introducing a photograph of the tissues of the victim Porteous and went on to show how he made comparisons of the accused bite marks. Prosecutor Chrumka then asked Dr. Swann to tell the court what he did to make identification.

"The first examination which I made in detail", the doctor answered, "was that of the study model and wax bites of the accused. During this time, I made notes of the details, which I saw on the study models in the articulate or closed position. The first characteristic, which I noticed in studying the models of the teeth, was the presence of a deep over bite. That is to say the front teeth on closure of the jaws do not contact each other at the edges when they are in a normal biting position." Dr. Swann then explained the discrepancies in Boden's teeth, such as worn and chipped enamel. How the teeth, when in a closed position, did not contact flatly together, but in some cases were off center. He then compared the photographs of the victim, showing how the discrepancies in Boden's teeth showed clearly on the breasts and neck of Miss Porteous.

Dr. Swann introduced two points of comparison, leaving no doubt as to the perpetrator of the violent crime.

On February 17th, 1972, Wayne Clifford Boden was found guilty by Chief Justice Milvain and sentenced to life in prison. On April 5th, 1972, Dr. Swann re-examined Wayne Boden at Spy Hill Correctional Institute. Further impressions were made. Once again, the suspect's teeth and occlusions (closed position) demonstrated a number of unique characteristics, which are reproduced on the study model and wax bites.

Dr. Swann's conclusion of his report on the death of Marielle Archambault in Montreal were:

> "The analysis of the concordant or agreeing points between the teeth and occlusions of Wayne Boden and bite marks present on the breast of the victim Marielle Archambault reveals 17 points of similarity. It is my opinion that this evidence clearly points to a positive identification of Wayne Boden as the perpetrator of this assault."

On Wednesday, April 12th, 1972, Wayne Boden pleaded guilty to three charges of murder in Montreal. He was immediately sentenced to life on each charge. The trial of Boden set a legal precedent in North America. Never before had a man been convicted of murder by the use of dental identification. Dr. Swann who had been asked to pioneer this type of identification in Canada had done his job well. He spent approximately 70 hours studying the impressions, charts and study models. He was then subjected to severe cross-examination by a very competent defense counsel. Yet, his evidence, that he had so meticulously gathered, held up. Dr. Gordon Swann played a vital role in bringing an elusive killer to justice. A killer who, three times before coming to Calgary, had vented his sexual desires on women while snuffing out their lives.

Cases of dental identification often include sexual attacks where the victim is not murdered. The identification becomes more difficult as the tissue of the victim is "live" and changes more rapidly. One such case investigated in Calgary involved a young man who had sexually assaulted and bit a 14-year-old female baby sitter. As a result of dental identification, the man was convicted. Presently there are three orthontologists in Canada acting as consultants to the Calgary City Police, RCMP and the Attorney Generals in both Alberta and Saskatchewan. Ms. Mary Hetherington, defense counsel, and Mr. Paul Chrumka, Crown Prosecutor have since been elevated to the position of Judge in Queen's Bench of Alberta. Our Justice system will benefit from their knowledge and society will benefit from the incarceration of Wayne Clifford Boden.

But the sentencing of Boden, as happens so frequently with hardened criminals, didn't close the case. Wayne Boden once again made the news on Friday, May 4th, 1984. The radio news reported that 'thirty-six year old Wayne Clifford Boden, while on a day pass from Laval Maximum Security prison, had eluded a guard in a downtown Montreal restaurant." I telephoned Deputy Chief Ed Madsen who had been on the senior investigators when Boden was charged with the murder of Elizabeth Porteous.

"Boden just escaped!" I said. "He was in a restaurant in Montreal and walked away from the guard. Can you believe that?"

"Boden is a smart man," Madsen said. "They may have trouble finding him."

Boden was arrested 36 hours later in a Montreal nightclub. Patrons who notified police had recognized the four-time killer. Boden had left his American Express Card (obtained after being imprisoned) back at the Laval Institute, thus blowing the theory that people won't recognize you without your American Express Card. Robert Kaplan, Solicitor General, said he was furious at Boden being allowed a day pass. Less than one year previous, in June of 1983, Boden had been refused parole, partly because the board felt he might kill again.

After Boden's escape, I spoke with a witness in the trial who had expressed concern for the safety of his wife and daughter. Other witnesses, many of them women, were at least safe while Boden was in jail. The situation changed entirely when he was allowed to walk away. Federal prison officials had felt the risk of letting Boden out of prison on a pass was "*almost nil*", despite what the parole board had said eight months earlier. Robert Caron, warden at the prison, said there had been no disciplinary problems with Boden during his twelve years in prison. That may be so, but while in prison Boden was under strict supervision.

That was not the case the day he was allowed to walk away.

CHAPTER THREE

By Reason of Insanity

"The courtroom gallery sat stunned. Sobs could be heard echoing through the otherwise silent room. Police officers sat staring in disbelief."

It was a beautiful June evening in 1971. Bill Gaskarth, my assigned partner and I were working afternoon shift. We were assigned to General Investigations. This type of assignment regularly exposed us to a variety of complaints from house breakings, shop breakings, and thefts. Periodically we were called on to assist in the investigation of more serious matters such as rapes and murders. Bill and I were both detectives. I'd been promoted in early 1970 while Bill had been promoted from Traffic Division several months before.

An extremely competent officer, Bill was assigned to traffic fatality as a sergeant. Traffic fatality was a unit comparable to homicide in the detective branch. Gaskarth's investigative skills made him one of the most competent partners I ever worked with. As we drove around south Calgary that evening, putting in our last hours of the shift and whiling away the time joking and laughing, the dispatcher's voice crackled over the cruiser radio.

"Unit 610, Detectives Gaskarth and Dubbin!" I picked up the microphone.

"610, go ahead" I said rather matter of fact.

"We have a housebreaking on Elbow Drive. Can you attend?"

"Shit!" I said under my breath "Ya, okay." I answered.

"Thanks," the dispatcher said, giving us the address. "we don't have any other teams available."

"No doubt" I said to Bill, placing the microphone back on the radio.

"Everybody else is at headquarters putting in their daily report sheet."

"Don't worry about it Bruce" Bill replied. "It'll only take us a few minutes. We can be out of headquarters before the other guys if we hurry. Bill broke into his unmistakable laugh. I began laughing with him. What the hell was I worried about? We got paid for overtime.

We found the address and drove into the driveway. The father was working near the garage. He came over to the car speaking to me through the passenger side window.

"Someone got in while we were out for the evening," he said glancing toward the house." I don't think they got anything but they ransacked my daughter's room. Seems a little strange."

"Let's have a look" I replied opening the car door and stepping out.

"Come on in" he said. "I'll show you where they were."

Bill and I followed the father into the house. As we entered, we were greeted by the mother and teenage daughter.

"This is my wife and daughter," the complainant said introducing us. "It was my daughters room they ransacked," he said as he showed us into the bedroom.

The sight before us was disturbing. Laid out neatly on the bed was an array of ladies' underclothing, panties, brassieres and slips.

The daughter laughed, "What would anyone want with my underclothes?" she said.

"Look" I said, "this may look comical to you but believe me from the looks of this, I would say you were very lucky you weren't home.

We may have been investigating something a hell of a lot worse than a housebreaking. By the looks of this, it's possible our friend has a sexual hang-up." Puzzled, the girl looked at her father.

"I agree" he said, "I don't think he came in for money. There are lots of things he could've taken but nothing else appears to have been touched."

"Yes" I interrupted. "I don't think he had stealing on his mind when he came in here. You're lucky you weren't home by yourself."

"I guess it isn't funny," she said apologetically.

"I agree," said Bill. "This looks like the work of a real kook."

We took the information, determining that the culprit had entered through an insecure kitchen window. Bill and I returned to the car, backed out of the driveway, and drove toward downtown. "Probably just some lovesick neighborhood kid." I said putting my notebook away.

"It's hard to say" Bill said. "There are a lot of nuts running round this city."

I picked up the microphone and cleared ourselves from the complaint. No sooner had I done so when the dispatcher called again.

"601, we have another housebreaking just a few blocks away. You're still the only team available."

"Why not?" I said sarcastically. "Looks like we're stuck for the night anyway. What's the address?"

Once again, the dispatcher gave us the address. Bill wheeled the car around heading back toward the direction we had just come from.

As we entered the second house, the father told us that the only thing taken had been some ladies clothing. The culprit had entered his daughter's room rummaging through her dresser removing some underclothes and placing them on the bed. The father expressed concern.

"The guy took some of my daughter's underwear", he said. He looked worried. We explained to him that we had just attended a similar housebreaking several blocks away. The culprit had also ransacked the daughter's bedroom, neatly placing her underclothes on the bed but taking nothing. Once again, we took the information and returned to our car. No sooner had we resumed than the dispatcher for a third time dispatched us to a nearby house. This time I was not sarcastic as I confirmed the call acknowledging that we'd take the call. Bill and I expressed serious concern as we drove toward the third address.

The method of operation was so similar to the other cases we could have used our notes from the previous two complaints to do our report. Once again, the housebreaker had entered through an insecure kitchen window going to the daughter's bedroom removing the undergarments and spreading them on the bed. For the second time, he had taken some of the clothing with him. Returning to our police car we once again headed toward headquarters. Our conversation became serious. We discussed the possibility of a maniac running loose in the area.

"This is one guy we better catch before he hurts somebody!" Bill said.

"Christ, can you imagine what would have happened if one of those girls had been home alone when he got into the house?" I said. "We would likely have a murder on our hands! Let's get our reports in and talk to the area car crew. They'd better keep their eyes open. If this guy is that active we could be in trouble."

As Bill drove toward headquarters, I lit up a cigarette and sat nervously tapping my fingers on the dash of the car discussing what our strategy would be the following day. The dispatcher's voice came over the police radio again. This time he was very terse.

"610 get out to Braeside. We've had a young girl attacked. It looks serious!"

The dispatcher gave us the address telling us to call him when we arrived. Bill and I looked at each other. The fears we'd discussed appeared to have materialized. I pulled the siren switch and reached down for our portable overhead police light. Opening the window, I placed the light on top of the car. We sped through the late night traffic not knowing what to expect.

The address was near the houses that had been broken into. The red light cut through the night's darkness reflecting on the houses as we sped down the winding road siren screaming. Bill swung the car into Braeside. We peered into the blackness trying to locate the address. With siren silent and red light off, we drove silently down the darkened street. As we neared the wrong side of the street, stopping in front of the address given to us, we rushed from the police car up to the front steps and through the partially opened door. We stopped in our tracks as we were met by one of the most bizarre scenes we had ever witnessed.

Sitting on the floor with her head bowed was a young girl in her late teens. I could see her reddish-brown hair and shawl were soaked with blood. As we entered, she slowly lifted her head. A towel that had been wrapped around her neck dropped slightly revealing a horrible gash. Her throat had been cut. Her lips moved silently unable to utter the words she wanted to say. Her horror-filled eyes conveyed the message she was depending on us to prevent death from snuffing out her young life.

"Oh my God!" the words fell from my lips unsolicited.

In my 16 years of police work, I had never seen a more devastating sight. Bill rushed back to the police car asking the dispatcher to rush the ambulance that had earlier been summoned. The girl's parents stood in the kitchen seemingly unable to comprehend what was happening. As Bill returned to the house, he handed the victim, Carol Marie Veregen, a piece of paper and a pen. We watched as she scribbled a description of her assailant and outlined the series of events that led to the vicious attack.

She then wrote, "I was walking home. He grabbed me off the sidewalk, held a knife on me, and took me to the park. He threatened me. I'm dizzy. About two inches taller than me. Blond curly hair I think around 20's, striped T-shirt. I think blue jeans. Please knock me out. I hurt all over." Again, her eyes searched our faces silently pleading with us to release her from her world of terror.

I stood up fighting back the revulsion of what we were witnessing. I picked up the phone and called headquarters speaking with Detective Les Goetjen of the homicide division. "We'll be lucky if this doesn't turn into a homicide." I whispered trying not to alarm the parents any more. "You'd better send a team out." I urged. As I hung up the phone, the sound of the approaching ambulance eased my fears. We had to get the girl to a hospital. I went to the door signaling the paramedics as they pulled up in front. As they entered the well furnished home, they too seemed taken back by the tragic sight they witnessed. Swiftly and efficiently, they administered medical aid to the young victim gently lifting her onto the stretcher they moved toward the door.

"We'll take her to Rockyview Hospital" they yelled as they ran to the idling ambulance at the curb. I stood at the door. The ambulance swung around with lights flashing and the siren wailing. It screamed off into the darkness. Detective Gaskarth came back into the vestibule as I was closing the door. He stood for moment wiping the side of his face. He eyes appeared lifeless as he spoke. He shook his head trying to fight off the tears that welled up in his eyes.

"I got most of the information from her mother." He said softly. "Her name is Carol Marie Veregen. She's only 19 years old." He said as his voice broke. Bill shuffled from foot to foot pushing back his red hair from his eyes. 'When she was on her way home from the bus stop she was attacked in a park at the end of the block.' her mother explained. "Looks like some guy followed her from the bus stop and grabbed her." He continued, shaking his head. "He threw her to the ground and tied her up with some clothes she was carrying in a duffle bag." As Bill wiped his mouth, he continued. "He raped her and cut her throat. I guess he thought she was dead when he left her. She managed to get free and crawl home." The strain showed on his face as he nervously tucked his notes back into his pocket.

Again, I phoned headquarters from the house advising the dispatcher the girl had been taken to the Rockyview Hospital. "Send the homicide team over there." I said exhausted from the frantic minutes we had just experienced. "Send us a K-9 team, lights to search the park and as many detectives and constables as you can spare. We better catch this bastard right away."

My horror had turned to hate and disgust. We spoke briefly with Mr. and Mrs. Veregen trying to comfort them as they prepared to drive to the hospital to be with their daughter. Detective Gaskarth and I left the house and followed a trail of blood down the sidewalk. It led us to the park gate where we lost the trail in the deep grass. Following the fence line, we soon found the spot where Carol had been attacked. The grass was trampled down and bits of clothing including the nylons used to bind the victim lay on the ground. Spots of blood could be seen in the thick grass.

The K-9 unit arrived, as did the night team of detectives and uniform personnel to aid in the search. Detectives Jack Taylor and Rollie Fisher from homicide arrived. They had been sent to the hospital but did not stay. Carol had been sent to the operating room immediately on her arrival. Doctors were working desperately to save the young victim. We later learned that a throat specialist from New York was in Calgary. He had been summoned to the hospital to assist in the life or death operation. He worked alongside local doctors attempting to restore the girl's speech.

Detective Gaskarth and I worked long into the night retracing Carol's steps from the bus to the park, carefully searching every inch of ground. Our eyes, tired from the long hours, scanned the ground. We picked up anything that might lead to a maniac stalking the neighborhood. Early in the morning, we returned to headquarters satisfied we'd done everything we could. We phoned the hospital and learned that Carol's condition was critical but stable. Bill and I put in our reports then exhausted and frustrated, we headed home. The rest of the investigation would be up to homicide.

Carol came from a religious home so we hoped that God would be on her side. As the days passed, we learned that Carol was improving rapidly. She had been taken off the critical list and was having visitors. Bill and I decided to go to the hospital to see her. When we walked into the room, Detective Sergeant Reimer and Detective Madsen were at her bedside. She smiled at us as we were introduced by Detective Madsen. She was as beautiful as we had imagined. Her long auburn hair fell cleanly over her face. Bandages hid the scars of her night of terror. Much to our amazement she was speaking. Choosing her words carefully, she greeted us. Although she was speaking, her voice was low and controlled. The operation had been a success. Only time would tell how successful. But Carol Marie Veregen, one of the bravest girls I had ever seen, would live to testify against her assailant.

The investigation continued for weeks. Several violent incidents were connected to Carol Veregen's attacker. A bulletin from the Vancouver City Police described an escaped rapist for whom they held Canada wide warrants. Kristen Francis Plough Kjeldsen had failed to return to prison after being issued a day pass. Kjeldsen's crimes were similar to the attack on the Veregen girl. Homicide investigators had reason to believe after comparing the description of Veregen's assailant with the description of Kjeldsen, that Kjeldsen was our vicious rapist. Several weeks after the Veregen incident, an elderly woman was attacked in her Southwest Calgary home. The assailant had entered the house through a basement window. The woman was struck by a lamp and found unconscious by her son. Identification detectives were able to recover fingerprints from a washer Kjeldsen had leaned on upon entering the building. The prints were rushed to headquarters and a file search made. Detectives were able to make identification. The prints were those of Kristen Kjeldsen.

As Homicide investigators intensified their search, further disturbing reports were received. A fourteen-year-old girl was indecently assaulted in her Southwest Calgary home. Numerous other housebreakings that were linked to Kjeldsen were reported. In late September of 1971, Constable Len Esler was assigned to investigate a housebreaking in the Britannia area. The culprit had been observed leaving the scene on a bicycle. Esler was armed with a police photo of Kjeldsen and two composite drawings done by Police artist Detective Ron Tarrant.

On checking a house across from the scene of the housebreaking, a woman identified the police composite of Kjeldsen. Not only did she recognize the composite, Kjeldsen lived in her basement suite. She went on to explain that her son had picked up Kjeldsen while he was hitch hiking from B.C. Kjeldsen had been allowed to stay at their home while he looked for a permanent place to live. On the day of the housebreaking, Kjeldsen was riding her son's bicycle. The woman told Constable Esler that Kjeldsen had moved that day from her home to a Haysboro address. Esler contacted Detective Ben Robinson, advising him of the turn of events. Robinson and Detective Bill Dalman rushed from headquarters going directly to the Haysboro address. The two detectives converged on the basement suite where they located Kjeldsen sitting on the bed. He was arrested and taken to headquarters where he admitted to Detective Dalman that he attacked Carol Veregen and several others he had been suspected of.

Homicide Detectives Madsen and Brink were called back to duty to interview Kjeldsen.

On arriving at headquarters, Dalman and Robinson advised the two homicide officers of Kjeldsen's admissions. Detectives Madsen and Brink entered the interview room where Kjeldsen had been placed. As they entered, the two investigators introduced themselves. Detective Madsen advised Kjeldsen that he and Brink were investigating the rape and stabbing of Carol Marie Veregen on June 13th, 1971 in the Braeside district.

"I understand you would like to tell us something about it?" Madsen asked. He sat with his arms crossed looking at Kjeldsen who was staring at the floor. Kjeldsen shook his head almost apologetically.

"Yes I do." He said without lifting his head. Removing his notebook and pen from his pocket Madsen leaned forward in his chair.

"Kris you're going to be charged with the attempted murder and rape of Carol Marie Veregen. Do you understand the charge?" Kjeldsen had his head in his hands and continued staring at the floor. He shook his head and replied 'yes' as he began his story.

Kjeldsen lifted up his chair and sat back. Pushing his hair back, he moved his feet nervously.

"I don't remember what day it was but it was in the evening around the middle of June." Kjeldsen rubbed his face hesitating as he looked at the two detectives. Once again, he shifted his eyes to the floor. "I was coming out of the Southwood area as I'd broken into a couple of places there. Actually," he said stopping as though he were trying to remember. "There were four but I didn't get anything out of two of them. I was walking toward one of the main roads when I saw this girl walking. I followed her about half a mile. Then she turned left on the other side of 14th Street. She walked a block south. I came up behind her, held a knife to her throat, and told her not to scream. I told her I just wanted her money. We walked together for a short distance into a park. I asked her for her money and she gave me some bills out of her purse." Kjeldsen lifted his head and looked at detectives. "Not much," he continued. "four or five dollars. I took some clothes from a bag she was carrying and tore them into strips. I told her I was going to tie her up so she couldn't get to the police. I tied her hands behind her back."

Kjeldsen hesitated as though he were trying to forget the incident. His eyes wandered around the interview room as though he were looking for something familiar. Detective Madsen pursed his lips looking over at Detective Brink who sat solemnly staring at Kjeldsen. Kjeldsen continued.

"I can't remember whether I cut all her clothes off or just some of them off," he said shaking his head. "I told her I would kill her if she made any noise. I raped her." he said matter of factly. "She then asked if I would let her get some clothes on and I let her put some on that she had in a bag she was carrying. I tied her up again and told her I was going to kill her. I stabbed her in the neck a couple of times. I thought she was dead so I left."

Kjeldsen sat back in his chair with his head down slowly wringing his hands. Detective Brink shook his head slowly and moved forward in his chair. Madsen set his notebook down, removed his glasses, and rubbed his eyes. He pushed his glasses back on.

"Kris why did you stab her and try to kill the girl? Did she scream?"

"No" Kjeldsen replied. "I just wanted to kill her. I didn't do it because I was afraid she would identify me. I just wanted to kill her!"

"Did you ever feel like killing someone else?" Madsen asked.

"Yes but I never did" Kjeldsen replied. He then told detectives that the knife he used and the clothes he wore on the night of the attack were in his bedroom. He then typed a statement.

Detectives Madsen, Brink and Robinson attended the Haysboro address where Kjeldsen turned the knife over to the investigators. He then took the detectives to the scene of the attack reconstructing the events of that fateful June night. Kjeldsen later gave Madsen and Brink a statement implicating him in an indecent assault on a fourteen-year-old girl in her home and the assault on an elderly woman in the Southwest home. He admitted breaking into approximately thirty homes stealing various items.

On March 29th, 1972, Kristen Francis Plough Kjeldsen was tried in Alberta Supreme Court on charges of attempted murder, rape and robbery of Carol Marie Veregen. He was also charged with the attempted rape of a fourteen year old girl and break and enter of her home where the crime was committed.

After the Crown presented its evidence, the defense called a local psychiatrist to the stand. The psychiatrist, after explaining Kjeldsen's mental state, testified that Kjeldsen was not capable of forming intent and did not appreciate the nature and quality of his act when committing his hideous crime.

"I know of no facility in Canada capable of holding Kjeldsen," he told the court.

The Judge adjourned to study the evidence. As we filed back into the courtroom after lunch, there was much speculation as to what penalty Kjeldsen would receive. Most investigators agreed he'd receive a life sentence. Nothing less would serve justice. Even as seasoned police officers, we were not prepared for the verdict the judge returned.

The courtroom fell into a hush as the judge was seated. After a lengthy summation of the evidence, including that of the psychiatrists, the judge turned to Kjeldsen. "I find you not guilty by reason of insanity. You are to be taken to a place where you will be held in strict custody to await 'the pleasure' of the Lieutenant Governor."

The courtroom gallery sat stunned. Sobs could be heard echoing through the otherwise silent room. Police officers sat staring in disbelief. We walked from the courtroom in silence. The frustration of police work showed on the faces of the officers as they left the court. Kjeldsen was sent to the Oliver Institute for the criminally insane. He was held for five years.

In the winter of 1977, Kjeldsen was released from Oliver on a pass to find work. He took an airline flight to Calgary. At the international airport, he hired a cab driven by Glenda Ferster. She was a beautiful blonde haired 5'4" 20 year old girl. He asked if she'd drive him to Banff. The young female driver agreed advising her dispatcher that she was on her way to Banff with a fare. She would be back by 2:00 p.m. at the latest. Late that night the cab company reported one of its cabs overdue on a trip to Banff. The RCMP was advised and an immediate search began. The taxi was found abandoned behind a Hotel in Banff. There was no trace of the young female driver. For two days, the RCMP and civilians scoured the Banff area, eventually widening their search to include secluded spots along the Banff highway.

Early one cold February day, searcher found the frozen body of Glenda Ferster. She had been murdered. Canada wide warrants were issued for the arrest of Kjeldsen charging him with murder. He was located in Victoria, British Columbia by two alert constables and returned to Calgary. On December 17th, 1977, Kristen Kjeldsen was found guilty of murder. He was sentenced to life in prison with, hopefully, no possible chance for parole.

CHAPTER FOUR

Black Friday

"The notes of the immortal hymn "Abide with me" echoed through the stately church while more than 300 mourners from all walks of life filed into the church and crowded the sidewalks and streets outside."

Friday, December 20, 1974 dawned bright and clear in Calgary. Little did anyone know that this day would go down as one of the most infamous days in the history of the Calgary City Police.

Detective Boyd Davidson and Philippe Laurie Gagnon lived two worlds apart but both would play a significant role in the tragedy that would unfold in the city known as the "The Sunshine City of the Foothills." Davidson was 43 years old with 23 years police service. He was a massive man, standing 6'2" and weighing about 300 pounds. His barrel like chest supported a 22" neck and a double chin. He left you with the impression he was scrutinizing you continuously while talking to you. An ex-junior football player, Davidson had been disciplined early to take on all tasks with abandon. His investigative skills were exceeded only by his tenacity. Such skills were displayed in the arrest and conviction of Lionel Llewlyn Staples for the murder of eighteen-year-old Robin Beynon. Her nude body had been found in a field in the southern outskirts of Calgary. The father of five children, Boyd Davidson took on part time work to supplement his income. He worked laboriously in the demolition industry, breaking scrap car engines with a sledgehammer. Davidson was a powerful man and he exhibited nerves of steel when it came to responding to dangerous situations.

Philippe Gagnon on the other hand, knew no bounds when it came to violence. Thus, the stage was set for an explosive confrontation. Curtain time came when Rose Demuelanaere, manager of the Ideal Grocery, eyed a man with suspicion as he entered her store about 9:00 p.m. on the night of December 19th, 1974. The man had been in the store before. Although she didn't know him, Rose felt uneasy when he came in. He was an unpleasant man, generally shabbily dressed, impolite and very curt. On this night, as usual, he wanted glue. Picking up six tubes he threw them on the counter, paid for them and left without saying a word. Rose wondered about the man. Was he sniffing the glue? His eyes were always red and puffy and he appeared to be frothing at the mouth. She was very wary of him. She decided that the next time he came in she'd call the Police.

The next morning at about 10:30 a.m., the man, later identified as Philippe Laurie Gagnon, returned to the store and purchased more Testors glue. As he was leaving, he turned and warned Rose. "If you call the Police, you're in trouble!" It was evident he was aware of her suspicions. Rose never answered, but the threat worried her. In fact, she was downright scared. But the man's caution now made Rose certain that this customer was sniffing glue to bring on a state of intoxication.

At 12:17 p.m. that afternoon, Rose ignored Gagnon's warning and contacted the police telling them about the man's actions, his appearance and her suspicions. Constable Harvey Gregorash was patrolling the area when the dispatcher called him to attend the Ideal Grocery.

"Report of a suspicious man," the dispatcher said. "See Rose Demuelanaere. She'll explain the situation."

"Right" Gregorash replied. "I'm just a few blocks away."

Gregorash pulled his car up in front of the little store and went inside to talk to Rose. Ms. Demuelanaere told the constable about the man's frequent visits to the store to buy glue and that he'd threatened her that morning. She handed Gregorash a sketch she'd made of the man. Gregorash recorded the information in his notebook, took the sketch and returned to the police cruiser. While he sat studying the sketch, he caught a glimpse of a man entering the store. Gregorash considered the possibility that the man was the person Rose expressed concern about. The constable waited until the man came out then took a second look. The customer fit the description. As Harvey was about to call the man over to the car Rose ran from the store pointing at the man.

"That's him!" she shouted. "That's the man who's buying all the glue!"

Gregorash threw the car in reverse, swung around the corner, and drove after the suspect. The constable caught up to the man and called him over to the car. Constable Gregorash stepped from the police car. "Come here!" he said. "I'd like to talk to you." The man appeared drowsy as he staggered with his eyes half closed. Constable Gregorash was sure the man had been sniffing the glue as Rose had said. He was frothing at the mouth and his face was red and discolored. The Policeman asked Gagnon to sit in the police car. The constable decided that if the man had been sniffing glue he could be charged under the Health Act. Suddenly the man dashed from the scene yelling, "I'm not getting in your car. There's no way. I'm going home."

The suspect ran down the lane and disappeared between two buildings. Constable Gregorash turned his car into the alley and began the pursuit. At this point, a motorist who had witnessed the chase into the alley stopped him.

"He's gone into a garage at the back of 1034—9th Street," the motorist said.

Gregorash approached the garage. It appeared to have been converted to living quarters. He knocked on the door but received no response. At this point, he requested assistance. Constables Dick and Linn arrived and were apprised of the situation by Gregorash. All three approached the garage. They knocked on the door and attempted to open it. They were unable to get any reply and the door was locked. Several times, they yelled at the suspect to come out, assuring him they weren't there to hurt him and that they merely wanted to talk to him.

Gagnon answered, "Come and get me."

Linn was at one end of the garage and Dick at the other. Gregorash was at the side and didn't hear the reply. Dick continued to check the garage, eventually finding an insecure window.

"I'm going in!" he said.

Opening the window, he crawled in removing his gun from its holster as he went. Gregorash followed Dick through the window. Dick noticed that the accused had shoved a desk against the door preventing access. Dick removed the desk while Gregorash opened a second door allowing Linn to enter. Inside they found what they had suspected. The garage had been converted into living quarters. In the middle of the garage was a pit, probably used at one time for greasing and repairing cars. The rest of the premises had a front room, a kitchen, a bedroom, and some modest furniture. Constable Linn peered into the bedroom and saw the suspect sitting on the bed loading a rifle.

Linn jumped back into the hallway as Gagnon got up from the bed, approached him and pulled the trigger. There was only a loud click. The gun had misfired. Cursing, the suspect moved back into the bedroom. As he did, Linn heard the suspect pull back the bolt on the gun and yelled to his fellow officers, "He's got a gun! Code 300!" A code 300 means a suspect has a firearm. A code 300 Red means the suspect is using the weapon.

Constable Dick crawled from his position toward the bedroom. Looking in he saw the suspect again sitting on the bed with the rifle in his hand. Once again, the officers heard a loud click. Once again, the gun had misfired. Constable Gregorash moved to the pit area and radioed headquarters.

"Code 300 Red!" he screamed.

Gregorash then quickly made his way back behind the desk located in the kitchen area. The constables knew they were in a dangerous situation and they had to get out. Constable Dick yelled at Linn to "Get the hell out!" Linn, standing near the southeast door, bolted outside. At the same moment, Gagnon moved back into the hallway from the bedroom and fired twice. Linn, standing near the outside door fired four shots into the wall near Gagnon. Gregorash jumped up from behind the desk and fired two shots. Gagnon turned and fired at Gregorash. A bullet ricochet from the desktop striking Gregorash above the right eye. He fell behind the desk.

Constable Dick yelled, "Harvey's been hit!"

As Gregorash crawled to the doorway, blood streaming down his face, Dick fired at Gagnon, forcing him back into the bedroom. The two constables then darted out the door. As they ran for cover Dick turned and fired again. As Constable Dick and Gregorash ran for cover, Gagnon appeared at the southeast door and fired again, striking Constable Dick in the right hip.

"I've been hit!" Dick shouted as he fell behind a fence.

Constable Linn, who had emerged from the garage a split second before, spotted Constables Barrett and Standish who'd arrived at the scene to assist.

"Get an ambulance!" he hollered. "Dick and Gregorash have been hit!"

Sergeant Ben Robinson and Constable Bob Whelpley arrived at the scene and took cover behind their police car, a scant 50 feet from the garage. Sergeant Robinson radioed for assistance. Other officers arrived at the scene and gave fire cover as Dick and Gregorash were taken for medical aid. Constable Dick was not seriously injured. The bullet had struck his wallet, stopping it before it entered his body. Gregorash had suffered a minor wound above the right eye.

At headquarters, Detective Boyd Davidson and his partner Lieutenant Fred Parker of the Fire Department were working the arson detail. This was a unit formed to investigate the ever-increasing number of suspicious fires in Calgary.

The two investigators had reported for work early that December day to prepare for an informal get together of the two department's top officials. Earlier in the day, Davison and Parker had spotted a car and occupants wanted for possession of stolen property. Thus, they were at headquarters instead of clearing up last minute details for the get together. They were scheduled to leave work at 2:00 p.m.

Davidson was standing in the detective office when he heard the call about the shooting in southeast Calgary come over the air. He learned that two Policemen had been hit. He yelled at Parker, who was standing at the other side of the office.

"Give me the keys to the car!"

Parker hadn't heard the distress call. It was 1:45 p.m. December 20th, 1974. Davidson, Detective Frank Mitchell, and Inspector Sid Coates ran to the police car. Their vehicle screamed from the garage heading toward the scene. The three officers arrived within minutes, taking up various positions surrounding the garage where Gagnon was holed up.

Davidson secured a shotgun from District Sergeant Farquharson, who moments before had arrived from the district office. With police car lights flashing and sirens screaming, a large number of police officers converged on the area from all directions. Some off-duty members were hearing the location.

Constable Kit Sylvester, a member of the support unit, heard the call from Sergeant Robinson and rushed to the scene with tear gas guns and canisters. With the assistance of Detective Davidson and other officers, Sylvester fired several rounds of tear gas into the structure. Deputy Chief Leary and Chief Brian Sawyer, who had been monitoring the incident, left the station to attend. Arriving minutes later, they took up separate positions with Deputy Chief Leary moving behind Detective Davidson as he slipped behind a neighboring garage. Sergeant Robinson continued to try and direct proceedings from his position behind his police car a few feet from the sniper. The situation became increasingly more dangerous as officers took up positions in crossfire situations. All police were aiming at the garage in a continuing attempt to subdue the deranged Gagnon.

As the firing continued and news reports went out, more and more civilians started gathering dangerously close to watch the drama unfold. Constables moved from position to position in an attempt to get a better sight of the garage and the gunman. Officers fired at will. Sergeant Robinson was unable to keep track of the many officers converging on the scene. He was pinned down in an area too close to the gunman to allow him to move. Some officers within close proximity of Gagnon were issued bulletproof vests. More shots rang out from the direction of the garage. Sergeant Bev Isaacs was struck in the chest while attempting to move closer. The bullet ricocheted from his protective vest saving him from a serious or fatal wound. Sergeant Mayer and Sergeant Farquharson arrived at the scene with more armament.

Detective Boyd Davidson moved to the northeast corner of the neighboring garage, firing from a shotgun in an attempt to allow officers to move into position to fire tear gas into the structure housing Gagnon.

Sergeant Mayer, Sergeant Isaacs and Constables Sylvester and Kubian moved to the garage where Davidson stood firing. Deputy Chief Leary moved in behind the officers. Sergeant Robinson and Sergeant Ogg, who had joined Robinson behind the police car near the garage, fired cover shots while Sergeant Isaacs stepped out from behind his cover firing several volleys of tear gas in Gagnon's direction. The tear gas wasn't having the desired effect. Gagnon remained firmly entrenched inside the converted garage. Shots continued to ring out from the garage. Some obviously, of high velocity, while others appeared to be from small caliber weapons. Several times, officers reported seeing Gagnon standing in the doorway firing with a 22-caliber rifle.

When it became obvious that the tear gas was not having the desired effect, more powerful weapons were used. Shots from an

M-1 automatic rifle were fired into the building, but again no apparent damage was done. Sixty odd shots were fired at the closed door in an attempt to dislodge it from its hinges. It remained intact.

Because the owners of the garage weren't home during the siege, an officer was sent from house to house in an attempt to find out more about the layout of the building. A neighbor who had built the garage was located. He explained the garage had reinforced walls built from boxcar siding and covered with stucco. The walls were almost impregnable. As officers continued to fire, Detective Davidson ran out of ammunition. Sergeant Mayer handed Davidson what he had and went for more.

As Davidson prepared to fire another volley of shots at the garage, a loud crack rang out. A bullet from a high-powered rifle penetrated the corner of the garage where Davidson and other officers stood. Detective Davidson and Constable Sylvester were felled. Sergeant Mayer returning with a supply of ammunition heard the anguished cries of Constable Smythe.

"They've been hit!" he screamed.

The time was approximately 2:30 p.m. on December 20th, 1974. Detective Frank Mitchell and Constable Garry Gray, seeing what happened, crawled to the garage door. Moving inside, they opened a large metal overhead door. As the door swung open they observed Davidson lying in a pool of blood. Davidson was still breathing. Constable Gray bent down and released Davidson's tie. The two officers then pulled Davidson into the garage. Constable Roy Evans rushed to assist Sylvester who had been wounded by the same shot that felled Davidson. Evans quickly removed his shirt using it to stem the flow of blood from Sylvester's wound.

As the firing continued, Constable Bob Barrett and Constable Standige were hit. Barrett got it in the hand and Standige in the chest and shoulder. Once again, officers set up cover fire, allowing paramedics to move into the area of the wounded officers rushing them to various hospitals throughout the city.

Away from the scene, Donna Davidson, Boyd's wife and her friend Francis Southgate, another Policeman's wife, had just returned from their children's Christmas concert. They sat talking in Donna's kitchen about the concert and Christmas being only five days away. Fran's two small children played under the gaily-decorated Christmas tree in the family room. Donna reached over and turned on the radio.

"Several police officers including a senior detective have been wounded in a shooting in southeast Calgary." the newscaster said, "The detective has apparently been critically wounded!"

"It's Boyd!" Donna screamed. "Please take the children and go!" she said to her startled friend.

Mrs. Davidson heard the news about the same time as Master Corporal Frank Lillies. Lillies, a member of the Military Police, was on his way back to Currie Barracks. He sped along the Crowchild Trail toward the army-training base.

Back where bullets whistled and canisters exploded, officers continued to be hit. From the protection of his patrol unit Sergeant Ben Robinson looked over at Inspector Coates and yelled, "Let's get a tank in here!"

Inspector Coates immediately conferred with Deputy Chief Leary. A call was made to police headquarters to contact Currie Barracks and request an armored vehicle.

Newsmen and spectators were moved back, but houses in the area hadn't been evacuated. Officers stood on balconies overlooking the garage exposing themselves to the accuracy of the gunman. Gagnon continued his sporadic firing from the garage almost as though he were merely firing to keep officers pinned down. As Frank Lillies entered the Currie Barracks Provost building, a phone call was received from police headquarters. An armored vehicle was needed to destroy the garage. The gunman had the police in a vulnerable position and several had been injured, at least two critically.

Master Corporal Lillies was the senior officer in the Provost building at the time of the request. Captain McMurray and Corporal Chauder soon joined him. Both volunteered to accompany Lillies in the armored vehicle. Corporal Chauder would drive. As the three army personnel entered the armored carrier, Lillies was issued a sub-machine gun for the protection of himself and the other two army personnel.

The carrier rumbled down Crowchild Trail with its provost escort attaining it's top speed of 45 mph. They were met at each intersection by police units clearing the way. It must have been an awesome sight as the vehicle rumbled to it's destination. Police vehicles with lights flashing continued their escort in an attempt to get the carrier to its destination hastily. Corporal Lillies, Captain McMurray, and Corporal Chauder discussed the firepower that the gunman had. Would it penetrate the vehicle? They didn't know. While they proceeded to the scene of the shooting the military men learned that more officers had been wounded. About 45 minutes after receiving the call, the carrier finally reached its destination.

Upon arrival, their first obstacle met them. Right in the path of the route they must take to hit the garage was an unmanned police vehicle. The decision was made that the car would have to be rammed and removed from its location. Once done, the carrier moved back out of the line of fire. The three army personnel left the vehicle to discuss the strategy with senior police officers. The carrier afforded protection for the men as they huddled to plan the attack.

A suggestion to have men follow the carrier into the building to capture Gagnon was quickly rejected when the carrier's personnel made it clear they'd be unable to see behind them. A second suggestion to have men sit on top of the carrier and drop tear gas into the building was also rejected. The army personnel were not sure the vehicle could not be penetrated by Gagnon's armament. It was decided that the only way they could successfully flush Gagnon from his position was to destroy the garage.

As army and police personnel stood talking, Detective Nick Graham arrived at the scene, taking up a position behind the patrol car that Sergeant Robinson was using as a shield. During Gagnon's wild shooting, Detective Graham stood up rejecting the shelter of the police car. At that very moment another bullet fired from the garage shattering the rear window of the police car and striking Detective Graham in the head.

Gagnon yelled, "I got another fucking pig."

Sergeant Robinson fell on the wounded Graham protecting him from further injury. He grabbed a T-shirt handed to him by a nearby constable and wrapped Graham's wounds. Robinson then assisted the wounded detective to a waiting ambulance.

I was back in the detective office continuing to monitor the situation, knowing only that the injuries were serious, but not knowing whom they involved. Some of the wives of policemen at the scene came to the detective office to wait for further news. Some were crying while others stood solemn-faced in disbelief at what they were hearing. At the General Hospital, doctors worked desperately over the still form of Detective Boyd Davidson. At the same time, Detective Nick Graham was being rushed to the same hospital in critical condition.

Gagnon's bullets were taking their toll. Doctor Young and his assistants did everything humanly possibly to save the life of Boyd Davidson. They failed. At 2:57 p.m. on December 20th, 1974 the veteran officer died of injuries received when struck in the back of the head by one of Gagnon's bullets. Nick Graham, however, would survive the ordeal.

The army personnel were told of Davidson's death and the danger of the mission became fairly self evident. Each volunteered to continue on as planned.

The operators climbed back into the vehicle to make the first assault. They were not given a police radio, thus eliminating the possibilities of outside communication once the assault started. The carrier swung around placing itself in position for the first assault. The carrier hit the corner of the garage at full speed. Roaring back, it made a second assault sending debris flying in all directions. The lumber and stucco fell on top of the carrier completely blocking what little vision the operators had. Again and again they hit the structure, each time the building could be heard to creak and groan as the carrier continued it's destructive mission. While backing up, the carrier ran over a police vehicle parked several feet away. Gagnon could be heard yelling inside the doomed building, "Come and get me army!"

The carrier made one final assault and in a cloud of dust and flying debris, the garage crumbled. Gagnon ran from the garage toward the house with a knapsack over his shoulder and a rifle in both hands firing as he went, obviously trying to reach the house located in front of the garage. Shots rang out from all directions. Gagnon jerked upright then went limp like a puppet on a string as the bullets pierced his body. Gagnon dropped to the ground still clutching one of the rifles. A police dog rushed to Gagnon's side grabbing the arm holding the rifle. It stood guard over the fallen man.

The siege was over. Gagnon had been hit twenty times. Six of the shots were fatal, including two to the head and four to the heart. A total of 65 shots were fired as Gagnon fled the garage.

As the firing died down, Inspector Ed Madsen was driving south on MacLeod Trail toward Ancourt Road, the home of Detective Boyd Davidson. Inspector Madsen parked in front of the well-kept bungalow. As he got out of the car he saw Donna Davidson standing by the front room window. Inspector Madsen rang the doorbell. Mrs. Davidson opened the door and said, "Boyd's dead isn't he?" as the tears streamed down her face.

Hugh Boyd Davidson was buried on December 23rd, 1974 from Bethel Baptist Church on 7th Avenue Southwest in Calgary. It was in this same church only ten days earlier that his daughter Kathy had been married to Constable Lawrence Wilson.

The notes of the immortal hymn "Abide With Me" echoed through the stately church while more than 300 mourners from all walks of life filed into the church and crowded the sidewalks and streets outside. As the service started, the Lord Strathcona Pipe Band played "Amazing Grace".

Detective Davidson was cremated and his ashes spread at his favorite hunting place, the hill of "Forget Me Not". Boyd Davidson's pretty wife Donna was presented posthumously with the Medal of Honor from the American Police and Fire Foundation for his courageous act and contribution to Fire Investigation.

Frank Lillies is now a constable with the Calgary City Police T.A.C team. He states there was no hesitation on the part of the army personnel to assist. They knew the possibilities of the carrier being penetrated by Gagnon's bullets. After making the assault on the building, the only sound they heard as Gagnon fled the doomed building was that of gunfire. Frank Lillies said, "It sounded like the third world war had broken out." The army had done their job well.

On the day of Detective Davidson's funeral, Corporal Lillies was assigned to escort the camp General to the service. After the service, Lillies met a number of Policemen who were involved in the shooting. It was during these talks that Lillies decided to join the Calgary Police Service. He did so on October 25th. 1976.

As a result of the series of tragic events, an inquiry was conducted. Deputy Chief Gordon Gilkes and a police commission member John Salus chaired it. On December 27th, 1974 a review board was established under the authority of the Calgary Police Commission and Police Chief Brian Sawyer, Mr. Gordon Gilkes and Mr. John Salus were selected to review the events leading up to the death of Detective Boyd Davidson and Philippe Laurie Gagnon.

Phase two of the report stated that:

> *"On December 29th, 1974 in Calgary, the limitations of the criminal justice system relating to the criminal psychotic became all too apparent in a sudden, violent and tragic fashion. A 26 year old man with a sixteen year chronology of victim oriented behavioral problems, blasted his way into dubious notoriety in a senseless, frenzied, drug inspired gun battle with police. The gunman's psychopathic behavior was clearly recognizable, starting as a juvenile runaway and ending as a convicted rapist. When mentally disordered offenders of recidivistic types are allowed to function unsupervised in society after their prison*

sentences are terminated, it is evident that serious deficiencies in the criminal justice system exist."

Gagnon had been a "serving prisoner" at the Drumheller penitentiary in Alberta. While serving time for rape and robbery, he had been released on *mandatory supervision* just a few weeks before the fatal shootout.

Mandatory supervision requires that a released prisoner remain under the *STRICT SUPERVISION* of his parole officer. From the facts presented, it would appear that Gagnon was indeed *not* under the so-called strict supervision he should have been. While in prison, Gagnon had displayed psychopathic behavior, which the prison and parole authorities recognized, yet they were unable to do anything about it before his release from prison under mandatory supervision. Treatment was only possible while he remained with the jurisdiction of the correction authorities.

Detective Boyd Davidson

CHAPTER FIVE

A Hostage For Your Life

"His calls for help had gone unheard . . ."

Staff Sergeant Keith Harrison and Detective Arnie Wilson sat in their police cars discussing a pending court case. Wilson was a recently promoted detective while Staff Sergeant Harrison was in charge of an area that encompassed the northeast and southeast section of Calgary. They were parked side by side only a few blocks from the scene of the infamous "Black Friday" shootout that two years before had claimed the life of Detective Boyd Davidson.

Keith Harrison was an extremely handsome man. He was square jawed and had dark friendly eyes accentuated by his deep tan. His smile was wide and his teeth gleaming white. His six-foot frame carried an athletic build. Harrison excelled in fastball and was well known in Calgary sports circles.

As the two officers sat talking, neither noticed a cream and brown Pontiac pull into the lane west of them. It bore British Columbia plates. Detective Wilson left the location telling Staff Sergeant Harrison that he was going to the district office to finish some paper work.

"I'll see you at the office later." Wilson said, driving out onto 13th Street and 9th Avenue southeast heading back to Forest Lawn.

"I'm going down to headquarters for awhile," Harrison shouted, "see you later."

Just as Staff Sergeant Harrison was about to leave, the voice of the Police dispatcher crackled over the police radio.

"All units, hold up alarm at the Inglewood Credit Union, 1300 block 9 Avenue southeast." Sergeant Harrison picked up the microphone,

"I'm only a block away," he said. "I'll attend."

Harrison headed west in the back lane toward the rear of the credit union. As he entered the lane, he observed a brown and cream Pontiac speeding from the scene. Staff Sergeant Harrison, still holding the microphone in his hand called the dispatcher again.

"I have a suspect car in sight," he informed. "They're going west in the lane behind the credit union. Can I have some back-up units?" There was no response from the dispatcher.

Harrison continued to follow the suspects' car out onto 12th Street, turning north toward the St. George's Island Bridge. Detective Arnie Wilson, now several blocks from the scene, swung his car around and headed back toward the credit union. Wilson was unaware that Staff Sergeant Harrison was following the suspects.

Staff Sergeant Auby Anderson, in charge of homicide and robbery detail, Detectives Hautzinger, Wenstob and Bain converged on the credit union. Harrison, still following the suspects' car over the bridge and along the zoo road, headed toward Memorial Drive.

The four occupants inside the suspects' car had noticed the unmarked police vehicle and its lone occupant. Twenty three year old John Gamble was out on bail from Surrey, British Columbia for murder. His sharp features accentuated his tall, lean figure. His dark, wavy hair added to his boyish features. He was dressed in blue jeans and a matching shirt covered by a black jacket. His garb gave him the appearance of a casual tourist. Dark glasses shielded his piercing eyes.

William Nichols was 37 years old. He was the oldest of the foursome. His blondish red hair swept down over his forehead. His casual attire was covered by a full-length trench coat. Although he didn't leave an impression of a hardened criminal, this man was also on bail while waiting trial for attempted murder.

Twenty one year old Janice Gamble, John's wife, was a 5'6" blonde. She was not only taller than the fourth member, eighteen-year-old blonde Tracie Perry, but had also had some exposure to crime; something Tracie was lacking. Moments before, John Gamble and William Nichols had robbed the Inglewood Credit Union while Janice Gamble had "stood six", meaning she'd acted as a lookout outside the small frame building.

John Gamble approached a cashier and handed her a note while pulling a revolver. The cashier quickly handed him a bundle of bills followed by pressing the hold up alarm. It was 3:17 p.m. March 12th, 1976. The two men ran from the credit union back to their waiting car, followed closely by Janice Gamble. The three of them cut between two small buildings leading to the lane where the 1976 Pontiac LeMans was parked. Janice jumped into the driver's seat while John Gamble and Nichols scurried into the back seat. The gravel-spitting car sped from the scene. Tracie Perry sat in the front passenger side of the auto, unaware of the robbery that had just taken place.

As the car and its four occupants left the scene, Staff Sergeant Harrison was pulling into the same lane. The Pontiac continued from the scene. John Gamble peered nervously out the back window. He noticed the unmarked police car.

"Get this thing moving!" he yelled at his wife. "There's a cop following us!"

Janice swung the car onto 12th Street over the St. George's Island Bridge and headed along the Zoo road toward Memorial Drive. Nichols and Gamble anxiously watched out the rear window. The police car was still following them. The suspects' car continued over the Bains Bridge turning left onto busy Memorial Drive. Staff Sergeant Harrison continued to follow the suspects. Once again, he called headquarters.

"The suspects are headed west on Memorial Drive from the Bains Bridge!" he said. "Can I have some back up?" The dispatcher did not respond to Staff Sergeant Harrison's call for assistance.

In the suspects' car, Gamble said,

"This is it. It's now or never." He ordered his wife Janice to "pull over."

As instructed, she pulled the car to the curb and stopped. Staff Sergeant Harrison stopped his police vehicle several yards behind the suspects. Harrison opened his door, using it as a shield as he cautiously stepped out. He drew his revolver, aiming it at the suspects, Harrison ordered them from the car. Nichols exited the rear driver's side, while Gamble stepped out of the rear passenger side door. Both held guns.

"Put your hands on the roof of the car!" Harrison ordered, "And put your guns down."

Nichols and Gamble complied, placing their hands and guns on the roof of the auto. Staff Sergeant Harrison left the shelter of his police car and approached the two men with caution. As Harrison was approaching, he stopped suddenly sensing something was wrong. He bolted for the protection of his car. In the same split second, Janice Gamble had moved from the front seat of the car to the rear, rolled to the passenger side door, with a gun in her hand. Nichols and Gamble grabbed for their revolvers and began firing.

Harrison stumbled, as he was unable to reach the protection of his car. He'd been hit. He staggered backwards, grabbed his car door, knelt behind it and returned fire. Flames spat from Harrison's gun as he fired. Nichols fell to the ground. Gamble ran to the side of the Pontiac, picked up his wife Janice and threw her into the car. He scrambled in behind her. Nichols struggled from the ground and into the driver's seat. As they sped from the scene, Staff Sergeant Harrison stumbled and fell to the ground.

Their cars lining the roadway, Calgarians stood horrified as the drama acted itself out before them. As Constables Greenwood and Fritz passed by in a Police van, they rushed to aid Harrison. As the suspects sped from the scene, Constable Fritz pursued them. He soon lost them in the heavy Friday afternoon traffic. Constable Greenwood ran to Harrison's police car and grabbed the microphone.

"Officer down on Memorial Drive!" he shouted. "Send an ambulance." There was no response.

Greenwood clicked the microphone again. The radio was not working. Throwing the microphone on the seat, he rushed back to Harrison's side, ordering a passerby to go to the General Hospital a few hundred yards away and send an ambulance.

Ed Zimmerman, a witness to the events, later testified that William Nichols fired the first shot. The shot that felled Harrison. As paramedics gently lifted Harrison into the ambulance, Detectives Norm Lund and Les Goetjen, homicide officers, arrived at the scene. At the spot where Janice Gamble had rolled from the Pontiac, they found a silver handled revolver. Blood at the scene indicated that one of the suspects had been hit. While the two homicide officers, Lund and Goetjen, continued their investigation at the scene, doctors at the General Hospital emergency ward were attending to Staff Sergeant Harrison. Sergeant Scott, a long time friend of Keith Harrison's, arrived at the hospital. He walked briskly to the emergency room asking to speak with Harrison. Entering, he saw Harrison lying on an emergency cot. Tears welled up in Sergeant Scott's eyes as he spoke with Harrison. "Keith", he said. "What kind of car was it?" Can you give me a description?"

Fighting back the tears of pain, Staff Sergeant Harrison whispered, "It was a '76 Pontiac, brown and cream. It had B.C. plates." The tears flowed from Harrison's eyes as he spoke. "I think I hit one of them," he said.

"Hurry," a nurse interrupted, "we have to get him to the operating room."

"You'll be all right", Sergeant Scott assured, visibly shaken. "You'll be alright."

As Sergeant Scott left the emergency room, nurses rushed Harrison to the operating room. Sergeant Scott met Detectives Lund and Goetjen in the hallway.

"Keith thinks it was a '76 Pontiac, brown and cream with B.C. plates." he told them.

"One of the witnesses tells us Keith shot out the back window." Lund replied. "They won't be hard to find. How's Keith?" he continued.

"It looks pretty bad." Scott said. "They just took him up to the operating room. He was hit in the side."

As the three officers left the hospital to continue the search and investigation, the brown Pontiac sped through northeast Calgary with its desperate passengers. Sighting a restaurant, Gamble ordered Nichols to pull in behind

"We gotta get this car out of sight!" he yelled. "The cops will be all over us."

Nichols swung the car behind the Thunderbird Restaurant. The four left the car, found a table in the restaurant and ordered drinks, sitting with their backs to the door. They discussed what they were going to do. Nichols got up and walked to the phone and phoned a taxi.

"Pick us up at the Thunderbird Restaurant right away." he ordered.

Slamming the receiver down he returned to the table. Without warning, Nichols jumped to his feet and walked to the cash register. He pulled a gun aiming it at the manager, Mrs. Javraj.

"Open the till." he demanded.

Mrs. Javraj opened the till. Janice Gamble ran over, scooped up the money and stuffed it in her jacket pocket. Mr. Javraj ran from the kitchen and was confronted by Nichols.

"You're both coming with us," Nichols yelled.

The taxi pulled up in front and the driver entered the café.

"Someone call a cab?" the driver asked.

"Yeah," Nichols replied. "Pull around to the back. We have some boxes to get out of our car."

The cab driver noticed the Pontiac's rear window smashed and wondered out loud what had happened. No one replied. Nichols forced his two hostages into the cab. The others scrambled in behind. Nichols and Gamble sat in front. A few minutes later, the taxi driver pulled into a gas station. While the driver was standing in the service station office Nichols stormed in.

"Hurry up!" he screamed. "I just shot a cop and I'll shoot you too!"

The driver threw the keys at Nichols stating,

"I'm not going anywhere with you!"

Nichols ran from the office, entered the cab and sped off. The service station operator contacted police. As the taxi swung onto 68th Street northeast, Sergeant Gerry Mayer and Constable Nail, cruising in a patrol car spotted it. Sergeant Mayer radioed the dispatcher.

"We have a taxi in sight with the four suspects believed responsible for the robbery and shooting" he said. "We're at 68th Street and 16th Avenue north east."

Several hundred yards up the road, Detectives Don deFreece, Ron Reed and Peter Jackson waited. As they heard the call from Sergeant Mayer, they spotted the suspects coming toward them. Driving just ahead of the suspects was a lone female occupant of an older Chevrolet.

Dianne Perry, a petite dark haired schoolteacher was on her way home from school. She was driving north on 68th Street northeast. Suddenly a taxi pulled alongside her car forcing her off the road. Before Dianne realized what was happening, Nichols ran to her car, threw open the door and ordered her to move to the passenger seat. At the same time, Nichols signaled the others to leave the taxi. Janice and John Gamble raced to the Chevrolet dragging with them their terrified hostages. Tracie Perry followed.

As the suspects sped north, the unmarked police car containing Reed, Jackson and deFreece pulled in behind. Sergeant Mayer and Constable Nail followed. As the two police cars continued their pursuit, Gamble pointed his gun at the head of one of the hostages.

The two police cars pulled back.

Nichols continued north on 68th Street. Suddenly he swung the car onto 22 Avenue and up onto a front lawn. The car doors flew open as Reed, Jackson and deFreece pulled in behind. As Nichols jumped from the car dragging a hostage, he aimed his gun at the three detectives' car and fired wildly. Detective Reed threw the car in reverse backing from the scene. As the suspects dragged the screaming hostages from the car, Sergeant Mayer and Constable Nail jumped from their police car, guns drawn and ordered the foursome to surrender.

"We'll kill all these fucking people unless you back off!" Nichols screamed.

A small child in a nearby house witnessed the bizarre events and yelled a warning to her mother. The mother hustled the children out the back door of the split-level as the desperate criminals forced the front door open and ordered the hostages inside. Mayer and Nail returned to their police car once again and radioed headquarters.

"The suspects have entered a house on 22 Avenue northeast! They've threatened to kill the hostages!" Mayer yelled. The dispatcher ordered them to move away from the house.

"We'll seal the area off."

Police units converged on the area, moving neighbors from vulnerable areas. A police command post (a temporary headquarters for assigned officers to work out of) was set up nearby. Inside the house, the hostages were bound and placed in separate bedrooms. Gamble phoned David Perry, Dianne's husband, telling him they had his wife and that they were wanted in Vancouver for murder and if their demands weren't met, they would kill the hostages. Gamble said he would call back and hung up.

Gamble then telephoned police headquarters. "Hello cops." The police dispatcher replied, "Yeah . . . ", there's a pause. Inspector Sid Coates was quickly put on the line to talk to Gamble.

Gamble: "Hello! Are you gong to talk to me or am I going to start wasting bodies?"

There was no answer.

Gamble: "Hello!" he yelled. "Are you going to fucking talk to me or not?"

Inspector Coates: "We'll talk to you. Don't get excited!"

Gamble: "I'll get excited 'cause I got dick all to lose. In two minutes I'm going to fire two rounds out this fucking window to show you I mean business and you'll do as you're told!"

Gamble left the phone and two shots were heard.

"Shots are being fired in the house!" an excited officer reported.

The officers were ordered to remain calm. They were told that Inspector Coates was speaking with one of the suspects by phone. William Nichols picked up the phone.

"Have you got that?"

"Yeah we got it," replied Coates.

Word was sent out to have Detective Hautzinger brought into headquarters. He is a trained negotiator. Inspector Coates continued to talk to Nichols while Hautzinger made his way to headquarters.

"Okay you listen closely." Nichols said. "We want to negotiate understand?" We know we shot that cop!"

"Okay" Coates replied.

"There's going to be a lot of people wasted if you don't do what we say okay!"

"Yeah! Go ahead."

"We want you to radio Vancouver, you understand?"

"Yeah. Okay!"

"Here's our names. My name is Nichols. I'm on bail from Okalla for attempted murder and armed robbery. My partner's name is John Gamble. He's up for murder from Vancouver. You radio them and ask about a break and enter and robbery on 10th Avenue in Vancouver yesterday and you'll find out where the arms (guns) came from. We have an M-1, an M-16 (automatic rifle) and a 9mm Luger (handgun). We have two 39's (handguns) and we have ammo. About three thousand rounds, so we are going to do it our way. We have fuck-all to lose baby okay?"

"We don't want anybody else hurt. That's number one." Coates replied.

Nichols responded, "Hey listen! If anyone gets hurt it's going to be your fault okay?"

"I'm sure nobody else will get hurt because of us." Coates reassured him. Nichols tells Coates that he does not want their names released.

"I don't care what else they get, but they don't get our names. Do you understand that? We have five hostages and we'll blow their fucking brains out okay? You got that?" (Nichols included Janice Gamble and Tracie Perry, their two female companions, as hostages). Tracie Perry, Nichols's girlfriend, was no relation to Dianne Perry, the third hostage taken. Nichols had one of the hostages brought to the phone.

"Help me! Just help me! I'm scared!" she pleaded.

"Have they hurt you?" Coates asked.

"No! They haven't hurt us." she replied.

Nichols left the phone, telling Coates he would leave the line open for further negotiations.

Detective Hautzinger arrived at headquarters and was advised of Nichol's call. Shortly after his arrival he received a call from David Perry, Dianne's husband.

"This is David Perry," he said. "I just got a call from some dude who says he's got my wife! What the hell is going on?" he demanded.

Hautzinger explained to David Perry what had happened.

"They told me they'd killed a policeman and they are wanted in Vancouver for murder! Is that right?" the distraught Perry asked.

"Yes! They are dangerous," replied Hautzinger. "We're not sure what they are wanted for."

David Perry pleaded with Hautzinger, asking him not to excite the suspects.

"I don't want my wife shot!" he cried. Perry was assured that everything would be done to get the hostages out safely.

Staff Sergeant Beattie and I were dispatched to David Perry's home to try and keep him calm. He wanted to go to the house where his wife was being held. We did not allow David Perry to leave the house.

Meanwhile, in the house on 22 Avenue North East, the suspects had become more and more edgy. Janice Gamble was concerned the police would find her fingerprints on the gun she dropped at the scene. Nichols picked up the phone and spoke with Detective Hautzinger again.

"How is the cop we shot?" Nichols asked.

"It looks like he's going to be all right." Hautzinger assured him. Nichols felt better. Nichols suggested that they wanted $100,000.00 in cash and heroin. Gamble can be heard in the background ranting and raving. Nichols assured Hautzinger that the heroin was for Gamble. He said he, Nichols, doesn't use it.

Hautzinger was caught off guard by the demands. All negotiators are trained to form a bond between themselves and the suspects. No demand is immediately refused. Everything becomes negotiable. Any concessions the suspects receive must be exchanged for something from them. Hautzinger told Nichols he must discuss their demands with someone in higher authority. Hautzinger left the phone and conferred with Staff Inspector Ernie Reimer and Inspector Sid Coates. It was decided they could not send in heroin. It is too dangerous. Something else must be substituted. Staff Inspector Reimer contacted a local hospital and spoke with a doctor used by the department as a resource person. Methadone, a heroin substitute, can be used. It will keep the suspects calm and reduce the chances of further violent acts. Staff Inspector Reimer made arrangements to have the doctor prepare several vials of methadone and needles. Like heroin, methadone is injected into veins.

Nichols was contacted and advised that the methadone would be sent to them in exchange for at least one hostage. An agreement was made. The doctor prepared the methadone and took it to headquarters. After further consultation, a vial was wrapped with needles and sent to the command post to be delivered to the house. District Inspector Penner took the package and cautiously approached the front steps. He threw the vials. The package landed heavily on the cement. Nichols opened the front door and retrieved the package. He took it back inside and telephoned the command center at headquarters, speaking with Staff Inspector Ernie Reimer. Nichols sounded very subdued. Nichols opened the package while talking to Reimer. Nichols cautiously removed the paper.

"I'm opening the package." he told Reimer. As he continued to tear the paper from the vial he screamed, "You've double crossed us. The vial's broken." Reimer convinced Nichols that was not the case. The vial must have been broken when it was thrown on the step. Reimer assured Nichols that another vial would be sent in to show good faith.

Although upset, Nichols agreed. The second package was delivered intact and Mr. Javraj was released. The two females remained hostages. The methadone did it's job. The suspects became less hostile. As night descended, an uneasy silence fell over the area.

The next day, Saturday, March 13th, negotiations continued. Nichols and Gamble demanded immunity for Tracie Perry. She had no knowledge of the robbery or how the guns were obtained. Staff Inspector Reimer considered the latest request. Investigation by Detectives Norm Lund and Les Goetjen had proven that Tracie Perry was not involved in the actual robbery. She had no criminal record. Reimer contacted Nichols and Gamble assuring them that Tracie would be granted immunity.

"Okay" Nichols said. "I want you to go on T.V at 8:00 o'clock tonight and publicly announce that she will not be charged." Reimer agreed.

That night he appeared on CFCN Television making the agreement public. Negotiations for the release of the final hostages continued. The suspects then demanded a large quantity of methadone. On delivery of the first package, one more hostage was to be released. After the final delivery, the remaining hostage, along with Janice Gamble and Tracie Perry, left the house. Detective Nick Graham and I were sent to the area. We watched from a house across the street as Mrs. Javraj was released. We then transported her to headquarters and obtained a statement. As staff Inspector

Reimer and Detective Hautzinger continued their negotiations, arrangements for the release of Dianne Perry were concluded. In the final demands, Gamble and Nichols wanted to be assured that they could remain in the house until noon the next day, which was Sunday, March 14th, at which time the police could enter.

Noon on Sunday passed with no word from the suspects. At 2:00 p.m. the TAC team fired tear gas into the split-level. Officers then stormed the house. Gamble was found dead as a result of an overdose of methadone. William Nichols was unconscious. The gun used to shoot Staff Sergeant Keith Harrison lay beside him.

Allan Keith Harrison, a veteran police officer, succumbed to his injuries on the evening of March 12th at 6:20 p.m. At 40 years old, he became a victim of the justice system he fought so hard to maintain. Two violent criminals charged with violent acts had been freed to continue their ways.

On November 22nd, 1976, William Nichols and Janice Gamble stood trial. Tracie Perry was granted the immunity promised. Her testimony helped convict her companions. Janice Gamble and William Nichols were found guilty of their senseless crime and sentenced to life. To protect the hostages, the death of Staff Sergeant Harrison had been kept a closely guarded secret. An inspection of Staff Sergeant Harrison's police car revealed a loose fuse holder. Though Harrison was able to hear the dispatcher and officers in other cars, he was unable to transmit. His calls for help had gone unheard—an unheard call which contributed to his death.

Staff Sergeant
Keith Harrison

CHAPTER SIX

He Died For a Dream

"1101," the dispatcher shouted to the district sergeant. "Shooting at the Pink Panther. Officer down!"

In the fall of 1976, Constable Shelever, tall, muscular and bespectacled, had realized a life-long dream. It was then that the dark-haired man was accepted into the Calgary City Police Service. The somewhat reserved Shelever was chosen at a time when the service was accepting only top candidates. At 31 years of age, he was late in realizing his burning desire to become a law enforcement officer. But the Yugoslavian-born welder proved his selection justified when he was graduated from his class with top marks.

His partner, 25 year old Jack Pedersen, was an ex Military policeman, having served in Egypt with the United Nations (U.N.) Forces in 1973. Pedersen left the military police and joined the Calgary Police Service in 1975. At 5' 7" and 190 lbs, he was an impressive looking police officer.

Shelever soon found that police work could at times, be tedious and unexciting.

There was of course the quietening of rowdy parties, checking traffic violators, arresting drunks, quelling minor disturbances in bars and so on, but on the night of May the 24th, 1977, 6 weeks after graduating, Shelever and his partner, Jack Pedersen came face to face with the brutal side of police work.

Prior to patrol, Shelever and Pedersen had been given a description of a young male wanted for armed robbery of a clothing store. Because this was a particularly quiet night Constable Pedersen and Shelever decided to check out some of the nightspots. It was in these spots where characters requiring periodic observation often spent their idle hours. Occasionally those of ill repute would pick up hookers who frequented the same spots, or they would just sit watching the strip shows for entertainment.

After checking several locations Pedersen and Shelever, decided to check out the Pink Panther, a popular nightspot. They entered the premises at 12:45 a.m. talking to the door-man as they entered.

The club was dimly lit. Only the flickering candles illuminated the faces of the few people occupying the sparsely decorated tables, or standing at the coffee bar. A small light over the coffee bar barely lit the evening menu of sandwiches and coke. Shelever and Pedersen stood at the door squinting as their eyes slowly became adjusted to the darkness. They scanned the room and Constable Pedersen's eye caught sight of a young man sitting at the counter drinking coffee. The man wore similar clothing and he had the same physical features as the one wanted for robbing the clothing store. Constable Pedersen turned to the young coat check girl, asking her if she had ever seen the man before.

"Yes I have." she replied. "He was in three nights ago but I don't really know him. He came in around 12:30 a.m. tonight and showed me a stamp on his hand indicating he had been in earlier tonight and had already paid. I was going to let him in for free," she said smiling and pushing her blonde hair back over her shoulders, "but he said he had been in three nights ago. I think he was just trying to impress me." she continued. "He paid and I let him in."

Constables Shelever and Pedersen stood casually by the door watching the show and the patrons. The doorman moved over to the coffee counter, standing beside the lone male, speaking briefly with him. The man later identified as Roy Glaremin spoke to the doorman.

"You ever do any time?" Glaremin asked. The doorman looked at Glaremin shrugging his shoulders and flicking the ashes from his cigarette, he replied,

"Yeah, I've done my share."

This seemed to relieve Glaremin; apparently believing he was talking to an ex-con, Glaremin tapped his foot and rubbed his face as he scanned the girls sitting at the various tables. Glaremin left the counter and moved from table to table. He spoke in low tones to the girls. He smiled to himself as he returned to the coffee counter. Leaning on the bar, he stood tapping his foot on the iron railing at the foot of the counter. It appeared to be a relaxed foot tapping, not one which revealed nervousness. Glaremin spoke briefly with the doorman again.

Shelever and Pedersen stood by the entrance discussing Pedersen's suspicions. At this point, Glaremin looked over and noticed Pedersen and Shelever standing by the entrance. Even while talking to the doorman, Glaremin appeared to be looking by him, watching the two uniformed officers as they stood near the entrance. Two plain clothed officers entered the disco. At this point Glaremin moved from the counter, walked past the two uniform officers and out into the hallway where he was out of sight of the officers for a moment. Several seconds later, Roy Glaremin re-entered the disco and walked briskly by the two officers at the door. He sat at a table with two of the club girls.

Constable Pedersen's thoughts kept flashing back to the robbery. Could this be the man? He called one of the plain-clothes officers over and asked him what he thought. Greg Park, the officer, agreed with Pedersen's suspicions. He felt the man should be considered a suspect and more checking done. Pedersen approached the doorman, asking him to instruct the suspect to come over to the door, as they wanted to speak to him. Glaremin never hesitated. Leaving his table, he approached the officers.

"We'd like to have a word with you for a moment if you don't mind?" Pedersen said. Glaremin agreed.

With Pedersen leading the way and Shelever walking behind the two, the three descended the stairs leading to the street exit. The doorman got up from the counter and sat with the two plain-clothes officers. As they were walking down the stairs Pedersen turned to Glaremin.

"Do you have any identification?" he inquired.

"No!" Glaremin replied. "I just came from Toronto today. I'm staying with a friend on 5th Avenue and 6th Street Southwest. I don't know the exact address."

He could give only a vague description of the apartment he was living in with his friend. As they reached the bottom of the stairs, Constable Pedersen instructed Shelever to watch the suspect while he went back into the disco. Pedersen spoke again with the coat check girl, confirming that Glaremin had in fact been in the disco several nights before.

Pedersen returned to Constable Shelever and the suspect. As Pedersen came back down the stairs, he noticed that Glaremin had a large wallet protruding from his hip pocket. Pedersen questioned Glaremin as to why he'd carry a wallet and no identification. Glaremin replied that he was carrying a large amount of money, but didn't carry identification because he was always being hassled by the police in Toronto. Constable Shelever and Pedersen decided to take the suspect to the police car and check him through headquarters to see if he was wanted, or if he had a criminal record.

Pedersen entered the driver's side, leaning over to release the lock on the back door, allowing Glaremin to enter. He then reached over to release the front door for Constable Shelever. Because the car had bucket seats with high backs, Pedersen momentarily lost sight of the suspect who was getting into the back seat too quickly, which indicated that he might not have been searched. Pedersen knew he hadn't searched him and both officers knew that a suspect shouldn't be placed in the back seat alone, certainly not without being searched.

As Constable Pedersen sat up he noticed through the split between the bucket seats that Glaremin was taking something from under the back of his jacket. When he was erect enough to see over the back of the seat, he found himself staring down the barrel of an automatic revolver. Shelever entered the passenger side, unaware of the turn events inside the police car. As he sat in the passenger seat, Constable Shelever looked back at the suspect. Just then, Glaremin cocked the gun pointing it first at Shelever then Pedersen.

When Glaremin first entered the car, Pedersen had ordered him to place his hands on his knees. However, as Pedersen leaned over to release the lock on Shelever's door, Glaremin had reached behind himself and pulled the gun he had hidden under his jacket.

Many times I and other police officers have done the same thing. Suspects have been placed in cars without being properly searched. I've attended a bank holdup, walking in completely oblivious to the fact that the culprit may still be inside. Only after the fact do you realize that the split second mental lapse could have snuffed out your life. The drama in the police car being witnessed by a number of persons leaving nightspots in the downtown area was created by just such a mental lapse. However, one spectator exhibited alertness and quick action. He immediately reported the incident. The following is an exact excerpt from tapes taken at the time.

Time: Approximately 1:00 a.m. May 24th, 1977. The emergency phone in police communications rings. It is quickly answered.

Phone Constable: "Police emergency."

Caller: "Ya police emergency?" This is John Snyder calling. I'm an ex-cop. There's a couple of guys outside in a police car. Outside the Paradise Gardens. There's a guy who jumped in the back seat. He's got a gun pointed at the cops in the front seat."

Phone Constable: "Paradise Gardens?"

Caller: "Right outside the Paradise Gardens. He's got a gun pointed at the guy's in the front seat."

There is a several second pause with no answer from phone Constable.

Caller yells: "There's shooting going on! There's shooting! There's shooting going on! Hurry up; get someone down here real quick. Send your Tack team. There's shooting going on outside.

There's no reply from the phone Constable.

Caller: "Okay I'm an ex-cop. I gotta get outside there okay?"

Phone Constable: "What's your name?"

Caller: "Snyder! John Snyder! I'm at the Tiki Tiki here. I'm an ex-cop. I gotta go outside."

Phone Constable: "No! Just hold on! Stay where you are."

Caller yelling: "You send some guys down here fast. There's shooting going. There's some police hurt. Please hurry up."

Phone Constable: "They're right in front of the Paradise Gardens?"

Caller: "Right out in front of Paradise Gardens."

Phone Constable: "Is that on the Crowchild Trail?

Caller: "No! Right on 8th Avenue and 6th Street. Right across from the Tiki Tiki. The Holiday Inn area."

Phone Constable: "All right just hold on now. We've got . . . (voice trailed off) Just tell us what's going on now."

Caller: "There's someone shooting outside. There was a guy grabbed a gun in the back of the police car. He shot the cop! Get down here quick someone get down here quick!"

Again, there is a pause with no reply from the phone constable.

Caller: "Please hurry!"

Phone Constable: "We got it. Just hang on. We got a car on the way."

Caller: "Someone please hurry!"

Phone Constable: "Just stay on the line please!"

Caller: "Okay! Bye bye."

The line goes dead.

The phone Constable hurried to the dispatcher to pass on the information. In such cases when the emergency line rings, the dispatcher is supposed to pick up the phone and listen to the conversation. He can do this without interfering with the conversation and at the same time, dispatch a car to the scene while the complainant is still on the line giving details to the constable. This apparently didn't happen.

The dispatcher later informed me that after the conversation, the phone Constable realized the severity of the complaint and went running back to tell him of the shooting. As Snyder stood talking to the phone caller, he was witnessing the tragic tale of events. Pedersen and Shelever were staring anxiously at each other.

Glaremin demanded they hand over their revolvers. Pedersen and Shelever shuffled nervously as their glances silently told each other not to surrender their guns. Glaremin was becoming impatient.

"Hurry up," he was yelling, "or I'll shoot you both right here!"

He kept moving his gun back and forth from Shelever to Pedersen.

"Okay" Pedersen said, "Just give me a second. I have to release the lock from my belt."

Glaremin seemed to accept this and waited silently while Pedersen fiddled with his flashlight holder, hoping to fool the suspect into thinking it was the gun he was detaching from his equipment. Glaremin looked nervously over to Pedersen and yelled at him to hurry up. As he did, Constable Shelever made a grab for Glaremin's arm holding the revolver. Because of the high bucket seats, he was unable to get a good grip and Glaremin broke loose. This time Glaremin screamed,

"I've quit fucking around! Hand me your guns or you're both dead!"

Meanwhile Pedersen had managed to release his flashlight holder. He held it in a fashion showing only the black of the handle. Glaremin believed it was the officer's gun. As Pedersen continued his charade, he purposely dropped the flashlight between the bucket seats.

"I've dropped it," he said looking at Glaremin. "Can I pick it up?"

Pedersen looked at Shelever attempting to convey a silent message that Shelever shouldn't struggle with the suspect. Shelever placed his hands on his head seemingly understanding Pedersen's message. At the same time he tried to calm Glaremin.

"Why don't you calm down and let's talk this over. Just put your gun away." Shelever said.

Glaremin appeared to have become more agitated. Again, he started to move the gun back and forth and yelled,

"If you don't give me your guns right now I'll kill you both. I got nothing to lose."

While Shelever was distracting Glaremin, Pedersen attempted to grab his own revolver. At the same time Shelever again, lunged at the suspect. Glaremin pulled back and Shelever missed. This time Glaremin placed the gun against the left side of Shelever's head. The gun was out of Pedersen's reach. The awkwardness of the bucket seats made it even more difficult. Realizing the life preservation action was now essential, Pedersen grabbed for his door handle and rolled out onto the street. Because of his concentration on escape, Constable Pedersen didn't hear the shot that took Constable Shelever's life.

Pedersen hit the sidewalk, attempted to stand up but slipped and again fell to the pavement. As he did, the suspect dashed from the police car. Pedersen looked into the police vehicle and saw his partner lying across the seat, his head against the passenger door. Glaremin ran to the back of the police vehicle.

Pedersen regained his balance and was standing with his back against the building that housed the nightspot that they had come from just moments before. Glaremin was only a few feet away. Pedersen had drawn his service revolver. He didn't fire for fear of hitting people standing across the street. Glaremin started to run toward the parking lot located at the rear of the building. As he ran between two rows of cars parked between the buildings, Pedersen raised his gun and aimed. Without warning, Glaremin spun around and fired. Pedersen felt a sharp pain as the bullet entered his left leg. He returned fire but missed. Glaremin ran to the alley behind the disco. Pedersen could see Glaremin silhouetted against the lights from the power station. He aimed and fired three more shots. Glaremin stumbled but didn't fall. Pedersen continued to pursue the subject but eventually lost him in the darkness of the alley and the protection of the parked cars.

Pedersen turned and ran back to the police car. Picking up the radio microphone, he yelled that an officer had been shot.

"I'm in front of the Pink Panther. The suspect ran into the alley at the rear. Get an ambulance over here!" he screamed.

Pedersen threw the microphone on the seat. He ran to the doorway of the Pink Panther and yelled at Park and Webster, the two officers inside. Because of the loud music, they didn't hear him. Pedersen ran up the stairs and again yelled at the two officers as he went. This time he gained their attention and all three ran downstairs, Pedersen explaining what had taken place. Webster and Park ran to their car, grabbed a shotgun, and entered the alley in pursuit of Glaremin. Police cars soon blocked off the downtown area, effectively blocking any escape route. Other patrol cars sped into the area to assist in the search.

"1101," the dispatcher shouted to the district sergeant. "Shooting at the Pink Panther. Officer down!"

The dispatcher continued to send cars into the area while the district sergeant shouted commands to the various units to take up positions. The search continued. The ambulance attended immediately, but did not move into the area of the injured officer.

"Get the goddamned ambulance down here fast!" came an order from one of the officers. The ambulance had stopped short because of a policy intended to prevent others from being hit during shootouts. While officers attended the mortally wounded constable, Pedersen, Park and Webster continued to scour the area behind the Pink Panther where the suspect had been last seen.

Soon the police radio carried a report of two officers stopping a person fitting the suspect's description less than two blocks from the main search area. Though wounded, Pedersen continued in the search with Park and Webster. When they heard the report of the stopped suspect, all three ran toward the police vehicle.

Nearing the police cruiser, Pedersen spotted the wanted man. The suspect was quickly surrounded by other police officers. Pedersen identified Glaremin as the one he was chasing after the shooting. Glaremin was placed in the police vehicle, handcuffed and rushed to the General Hospital suffering from gunshot wounds. Pedersen was taken to another police car and transported to the Holy Cross Hospital. Constable Shelever was removed to the ambulance and rushed to the Holy Cross Hospital at approximately 1:10 a.m. where emergency surgery was started.

Dr. Barlass, a neuro-surgeon at the Holy Cross Hospital performed the delicate operation. Shortly after 3:00 a.m., Shelever was transferred to the intensive care unit. Constable William Shelever, a rookie officer with the Calgary Police Service, had seen a lifetime dream come true when the Calgary Police Service accepted him. Little did he know that in a few short weeks of active duty he would be one of the many victims of today's violent society.

In the early morning of May 26th, 1977, Constable Shelever died. Investigation of the suspect Roy Glaremin showed that he and two accomplices were wanted in Edmonton for armed robbery. The gun used to kill Constable Shelever had been stolen during a break in of an Edmonton sporting goods store. His accomplices in the Edmonton robbery returned to that city and surrendered to police. A letter from Glaremin's mother led to speculation that he was from a broken home. Glaremin was arrested within an hour of roadblocks being set up. Suffering from gun shot wounds inflicted when Constable Pedersen returned fire near the Pink Panther, Glaremin was taken to hospital. On December 21st, 1977, Glaremin was found guilty of first-degree murder in the shooting death of Constable Shelever. Though sentenced to life imprisonment with no parole for 25 years, the Criminal code allows convicted killers to apply to the Chief Justice in the province of conviction for a hearing to have the 25 years with no parole reduced or terminated.

Constable William Shelever

CHAPTER SEVEN

I'd Bet My Life

"I cannot help but wonder why Bloome was allowed to operate unmolested for so many years."

In February of 1977, I was assigned to head up the Morality Unit under the direction of Inspector Auby Anderson. After meeting with him on the unit's priorities, it was decided that we would be targeting massage parlors, social club gambling and bookmaking.

Allan Louis Bloome (pronounced Bloomie), an ex-biker, controlled the massage parlor industry, operating Sultan's Palace, Tahiti Retreat, Golden Girls and Neptune' Hideaway.

All were massage parlors catering to the sexual needs of the customers. Bloome had been operating for approximately three years virtually unmolested. He had risen from the ranks of the Grim Reapers motorcycle club to become head of the Calgary massage parlor business specializing in the service of prostitutes. Gambling was also operating at will. Five so-called "social clubs" had made a profitable business out of catering to the gamblers. The five clubs, Sportsman's Association, Playfair Club, Ben Brotherhood Club, Code Six and the Stockman's Library Association had been operating under a social charter.

Chinatown, well known for its back room gambling had been operating since I joined the police department in 1955. In all my years on the job, I could not recall Chinatown ever having been "busted" for illegal gambling. Bookmaking, a multi-billion dollar a year business in Canada, had several major connections in Calgary. In the past, it appeared as though only 'cosmetic' raids were done on the Calgary gambling scene. Morality had a reputation of being a "dangerous" unit to work. In the past, detectives had been fired, demoted, or charged with discreditable conduct as a result of their association with pimps, prostitutes and gamblers. Because of this, many detectives preferred not to work the unit. I was not concerned. The members who were working the unit when I took over were competent professional Policemen who I felt I could rely upon. I felt that I had the integrity to keep a safe distance from the criminal element, yet still communicate with them.

In spite of my confidence, it was not long before members of the unit advised me that local gamblers were asking what kind of liquor I drank and what kind of cigarettes I smoked. My first Christmas as morality staff sergeant made me realize how easy it was to become entangled in the complicated world of payoffs. Answering my door one evening, I was greeted by a retired politician carrying a large box. The box contained a dozen or more bottles of the most expensive liquor.

"Merry Christmas Bruce!" he said as he thrust the box into my arms. "Just a little gift for Christmas."

"What the hell is this?" I said, startled at his appearance at my front door.

"Take this in the spirit in which it is given." he said as he left.

Turning and walking back into my front room, I showed my wife the 'gift'.

"I guess it comes with the territory" I said putting the box down. I immediately telephoned Superintendent Reimer, advising him that I would be returning the gift in the morning. The incident had scared me. What had I done to make anyone believe that I would accept anything from the people I had to deal with?

Our unit started its first major operation in February of 1977. Our target was the gambling Establishments. After weeks of observation, we struck on March 10th. We raided the five clubs, seizing over $100,000.00 worth of chips and money. Accounting books seized at the time indicated the clubs were running a profitable business. An audit later confirmed our suspicions. In all we arrested 51 operators and players. The courts, realizing the severity of the gambling problem, imposed fines up to $10,000.00. Gaming operators, who had, in the past, greeted Policemen entering the premises, now barred the door. Tension between the police and gamblers increased over the next several months, with some operators accusing morality officers of lying during testimony.

On January 14, 1978 we completed one of the most difficult operations in gambling. Chinatown. Though for years morality detectives had stood watching the Chinese games, few, if any, understood the games sufficiently enough to conduct a successful prosecution. Detectives Roger Boiteau and Ken Sprouse, whom I had assigned to gambling detail, took on the task of learning about the games being played in the dimly lit back rooms in Chinatown. Both had taken courses in Chinese gambling and now must familiarize themselves with our local element. For weeks, night after night, they entered the gambling premises, questioning players on the complexity of the games being played. Fan Tan, Chinese Lottery, Pie Gau and Mah Jong were some of the more popular games played nightly in Chinatown.

Once we had gathered sufficient evidence for court, we struck. Taken by surprise, the gamblers stood staring in disbelief as the contingent of policemen, led by Boiteau, Sprouse and myself, swarmed into the room seizing gambling paraphernalia, record books and equipment. An identification detective moved swiftly from table to table, taking pictures of the operators and players alike. As Detectives Boiteau said later, "We took everything but the light fixtures."

For the first time in my 22 years as a Policeman, Chinatown gambling establishments had been raided. In the months prior to our raids, I had received many phone calls from concerned relatives of gamblers. Many of the men spent all night gambling, often losing thousands of dollars. Books seized during the raids, and later audited by a chartered accountant, indicated that operators of the games were making as much as $1 million a year in profit. Fan Tan, a popular Chinese game is played with buttons.

A rectangle is set up in the middle of the table with positions one, two, three and four. The players bet on which position will win. The operator then scoops up a handful of buttons and places them under a lid. The buttons are then removed four at a time. The player who has the correct number remaining at the end wins. The rest of the players lose their bet to the operator.

Court preparation took months. The complicated systems used by the Chinese had to be clearly explained to a judge unfamiliar with such games. Judge John Harvie, after listening to days of evidence, found two of the operators guilty, fining each of them $10,000.00. Large by some standards, but paltry compared to the profits realized by the owners. During the raids, we seized $40,000.00 in cash. One elderly Chinese Gentlemen was found to have $18,000.00 cash in his pocket. The local news media were very critical of our operation, accusing us of infringing on a Chinese tradition that hurt no one and was restricted to the Chinese community.

In my thirty months as morality sergeant, I discovered that most of our operations were unpopular. Gambling and prostitution, like apple pie, was enjoyed by a large segment of the population. Very often that segment consisted of influential people. The once friendly Chinese community was now very distant. No longer were the operators of the cafes and posh restaurants that lined Centre Street friendly. Once again, we had made an enemy.

In our continuing fight against gambling, we homed in on the local bookmakers, one of the most lucrative businesses in the country. We knew that local charges would not stop the industry, but at least we could let them know that they'd not operate with a free hand unmolested. A newspaper report from Toronto on January 21, 1979, reported the following:

> *"The Globe and Mail says more than $10 million in illegal bets in Toronto will be riding on the outcome of today's Super Bowl Football game."*

The newspaper quotes sources with the Metropolitan Toronto police and with the provincial police as saying illegal wagering, of which at least $500 million is done each year in Toronto, is a big moneymaker for organized crime. Of about 200 bookmakers in Toronto, 25 to 30 are big volume operators who do at least $75,000.00 a week in action, a police intelligence source is quoted as saying. The newspaper also quotes police sources as saying that more than $2 billion was wagered illegally with bookmakers on sports events in Canada last year, at least $1 billion of which was bet in Ontario. By Comparison, the newspaper says that in 1976 only four Canadian-controlled industries—Canadian Pacific Ltd., Inco Ltd., Bell Canada Ltd. and Massey Ferguson Ltd. recorded more than $2 billion in sales. Bookmakers have a country wide network. Anything we did in Calgary had an effect on bookmakers in other parts of the country. Police agencies in other Canadian cities had, in years gone by, expressed concern over Calgary's handling of bookmakers. Allegation were made during a nationwide crack-down on bookmakers that Calgary morality officers had "tipped off" the bookmakers when there was going to be a raid, allowing them time to prepare.

Once we started our operation on the bookmakers, we worked swiftly, gathering evidence by telephone interception and by sending plainclothes constables into beer parlors and lounges to act as prospective customers. Our success was instant. Bookmakers who had operated freely in the past now felt the sting of our operation. Seldom had they been subjected to such intense investigation. Again, the courts reacted positively, fining the bookmakers heavily. But like prostitution, we had merely slowed down the lucrative business. Slowly but surely, the bookmakers resurfaced to once again enjoy the profits of their business.

Inspector Auby Anderson and I had discussed the massage parlor problem many times. In early 1977 we decided, after consultation with members of the morality unit, that taking down the massage parlors and convicting Allan Louis Bloome would be a monumental task. We must be well prepared and able to carry on the operation for months if necessary. Our unit must be bolstered with additional men and equipment. Inspector Anderson and I spoke with Burt Andersen, a city licensing officer, who had for months attempted to close Bloome's operations down by charging him with operating without a license. Bloome simply ignored the summons and continued to operate.

In 1976, Burt Andersen had obtained a Supreme Court injunction against Bloome to have the parlors closed. Lawyers fighting for Bloome appealed decision after decision and the parlors continued to operate.

"The only way you'll close down Bloome's operation," Burt Andersen said, "is to charge him with living off the avails of prostitution. He sure as hell isn't going to close down for us."

In the weeks that followed, Inspector Anderson and I met with Superintendent Reimer, outlining our concerns. Reimer immediately bolstered the morality unit with extra men. Criminal Intelligence Unit, a special crimes unit, obtained court orders allowing us to monitor Bloome's telephones, the telephones to the massage parlors and all other principals involved. I assigned Detective Rick Talbott to head up the operation. We then systematically watched Bloome's four parlors. Detectives and plainclothes constables alike, sat in unmarked police cars, watching the stream of customers entering and leaving the sex shops. Detective Brian Olson headed up the surveillance squad, watching clients at massage parlors and subsequently stopping them to obtain names and addresses.

Once the customer was a safe distance from the parlor, we would have them stopped by a uniformed officer who would obtain names and addresses. Not surprising to us, many of the customers were people from the upper class. While doing our surveillance, we observed a chief of police from a city outside Alberta, a lawyer, a doctor, an airline pilot, and a judge.

The Judge was seen sitting in the reception room of one of the parlors. Many of the other customers were executives from other walks of life.

What had apparently been obvious to other members of the morality squad for years was now becoming apparent to me. Bloome was rapidly becoming a millionaire through the operation of the four sex shops. He drove an expensive Lincoln and lived in a $600,000.00 home in the suburbs. Bloome had established a number of phony companies to launder his money (putting money obtained through the massage parlors into other businesses). It was through these companies that he was able to obtain the use of a major credit card company machine so his customers could pay by credit card. One man using his credit card to pay for services rendered at a massage parlor, wrote neatly on the bottom of the slip "for installation of new motor."

During the operation, we worked closely with Sergeant Harry Smelgis of the RCMP Commercial Crime Unit and members of the Income Tax Division. All accompanied us on the day of raids. As the evidence continued to mount, we were able to connect Bloome to the prostitution end of the business. We learned that Bloome charged each of the girls $50.00 a day to work for him. The girls would charge the customer $35.00 an hour for an encounter session. All of this money also went to Bloome. The girls would later testify that they made their money on "tips". Customers wanting sexual favors would bargain with the girls on price. Sexual favors included oral sex, masturbation, intercourse, reverse massage, (the customer massaged the girl) or Swedish massage, which was being massaged in baby oil. One telephone call we intercepted between two of Bloome's girls vividly described a lesbian encounter with a female customer. Obviously a profitable business, books seized from one of the girls during the raids indicated she had made eighty-six thousand dollars in little over a year.

On May 10, 1977, we struck. Over sixty members of the Calgary City Police, R.C.M.P. and Income Tax investigators were involved in the raids. Detective Talbott had made up search and seizure and arrest warrants for Bloome, the girls and other principals involved. Bloome's four parlors, his home, his banks, and the home of each of the girls, were raided. R.C.M.P. officers in Saskatchewan raided homes in that area. Calgary news media later described the raids, as one of the largest in Western Canada's history.

Bloome was arrested at his posh suburban home, while the girls were arrested in various locations in Calgary.

Later that day, all were released to appear in court again the following day. After court on May 11, Bloome held a luncheon for the girls at a local restaurant. After the lunch, Bloome threatened the girls, stating "they would be swimming" if they testified against him. On hearing of the threats, we again arrested Bloome, charging him with obstruction. The courts released him on bail, advising him not to associate with any of the girls. Nine times during our investigation, Bloome would be arrested on various criminal charges. Each time he was released on bail.

During the operation, threats of death were made against Detective Ken Sprouse and myself. We were told that the criminals in Calgary felt that I had been too zealous in my investigation. Though no one was ever charged with the threats, Detective Sprouse and I were ordered to draw shotguns from our stores and carry them while going to and from work. It has been alleged our assassination would be carried out while we were going to or from work. While off duty, I carried my service revolver with me at all times. The department made arrangements to have Sprouse and myself followed by our surveillance team to protect us from any attempts on our lives. Many nights at my home, while my wife and six children were asleep, I would sit in the front room, lights off, watching and listening for unusual noises or the sound of passing cars. While out shopping with my family, I would scan the crowd looking for the unknown enemy. Often while driving to work, I would feel the hair on the back of my neck tingle as a car or motorcycle pulled up alongside me.

Within a week of our initial raids, the four massage parlors were back in operation. In August of 1977, our Special Crimes Unit again raided the parlors and again charged Bloome with living off the avails of prostitution. Again, the courts released him.

In the spring of 1978, Bloome was sentenced to four years for living off the avails. In December of 1978, he received an additional four years for obstructing justice by threatening the girls. In the spring of 1979, he received an additional year on the second charge of living off the avails. All terms were to run consecutively. Bloome was moved from prison to prison in his first three years, ending up at Stony Mountain Institute, a medium security prison in Manitoba.

In June of 1981, he was transferred to the minimum-security prison of Rockwood, near Winnipeg. Though in 1980 he was refused parole, Bloome was granted a five-day pass in August of 1981. He was to come to Calgary to clear up some legal matters. Bloome never returned to the prison.

On February 15, 1984, U.S. Marshals arrested Bloome as he was leaving a motel in Snowflake, Arizona. When arrested, Bloome had a revolver stuffed under his belt. James Click, one of the arresting officers from the Navajo County Sheriff's office stated that "before Bloome put his hands up, he seemed to go for his gun on three occasions. If I ever arrested a man with a death wish who wanted us to blow him away, it was Bloome". A search of Bloome's vehicle turned up 112 grams of pure cocaine, valued at $180,000.00 on the street. In the pocket of Bloome's well-tailored suit was $3,800.00 in $100 bills. When arrested, Bloome was driving a truck and a lady friend with him at the time was driving a Lincoln registered to Bloome. At 38, Allan Louise Bloome was still a handsome, soft-spoken articulate man. Dubbed the Sultan of Sleaze by some reporters, he rose through the ranks of the Grim

Reapers Motorcycle Club to become the King of the massage parlor chain in Calgary. As Frank Dabbs and Rick Dolphin, reporters for the Alberta Report wrote in an article dated March 5th, 1984:

"Bloome kept a high profile, mixing with journalists and politicians as the self appointed spokesman for the massage industry." I cannot help but wonder why Bloome was allowed to operate unmolested for so many years. Why was he allowed to become so successful before the raids of May 10, 1977?

CHAPTER EIGHT

Portrait of a Criminal

"Friend . . . or foe?"

I first met Harry Murphy in early 1971. Like most Calgary Policemen, I had often heard Harry's name associated with crime. If there was a major break-in, Harry did it. If there was an armed robbery, Harry did it. Regardless of the type of unsolved crime that plagued our department, you could be assured that someone would say "Harry did it." I started to think that Harry was a one-man crime machine.

At age 27, Harry Martin Murphy was an ominous figure of a man. He stood 5'10" and was barrel-chested sporting a dark beard. His hair was thick and wavy, and as black as his leather jacket. Harry Murphy was the picture of a stereotypical criminal. Murphy always wanted to become a policeman. When he was unsuccessful, he became a criminal . . . a professional criminal.

My partner, Carl Gerrard, had recently been promoted to the detective division. He was a red-headed, quick-witted man who would often jokingly take credit for my own two red-headed children. One morning, Carl Gerrard and I were assigned to keep under surveillance a truck that had been used in a shop breaking and theft at a local warehouse. Constable Bev Isaacs watched the truck during the night, which had been located several hours after the break and enter. We left the station early that morning to set up our surveillance of the truck. It was parked a short distance from a school.

Before leaving the station, we were cautioned that Murphy was a dangerous individual and may very well be carrying a gun. Carl and I checked our guns as we left the station, making sure they were loaded.

We spoke briefly with Constable Isaacs on our arrival at the location, obtaining what information he had. We took up our position several hundred yards from the truck, keeping it in sight. At about 8:00 a.m. we were joined by Detective Ben Robinson and Russ Bain. They took up a position several hundred yards on the other side of the truck. Escape routes were now effectively blocked off. At about 8:30 a.m. we noticed Harry Murphy's black Lincoln cruising the area. There were three males in the car. Harry was driving. We contacted Robinson and Bain who had also seen the car.

"Don't jump them until they get in the truck." Robinson cautioned. "We don't want to lose them. And be careful." he warned.

Instinctively, I felt for my gun, assuring myself it was still there.

The Lincoln circled the block several times before stopping a half a block from the truck. We watched as a passenger left the Lincoln. Looking around, he walked toward the truck. "Now! Now!" I thought. "This is it. The minute the truck starts moving we got them." As the man reached the truck, he grabbed the door handle, took another look around and swung himself up on the running board. Swinging the door open, he slid in behind the wheel. I could hear my heart pounding as we waited and waited. Nothing was happing. The truck wouldn't start!

"For Christ sakes" Carl whispered. "Don't tell me they can't get the bloody thing going?"

As we watched, Murphy got out of the Lincoln and walked toward the truck. He opened the truck door and swung in. Nothing! Murphy left the seat, opened the truck hood and worked on the engine for a moment. He then signaled the man in the truck. In a second the engine was roaring. Murphy closed the hood and sauntered back to his car. As the truck started moving, Carl picked up the microphone.

"Let's move in", he said to Robinson and Bain. "We'll take the Lincoln if you take the truck." Carl said.

"Right!" they replied. I started our car and moved it slowly toward the Lincoln.

"Let's go!" Carl yelled.

I accelerated the police car. Robinson and Bain, now in sight, were heading toward the truck. Carl drew his revolver as I pulled the police car along side the Lincoln, blocking it off. It was then I got my first look at Harry Murphy, the criminal extraordinaire. Carl jumped from the police car, aiming his gun directly at the heavyset man behind the wheel. The two occupants placed their hands on the dash.

"Out!" Carl ordered. "Out!"

Harry Murphy opened the car door and slowly slid out, placing both his hands on his head. I left the police car and walked around to the passenger side of the Lincoln. With my gun drawn, I ordered the second man from the car. We handcuffed our prisoners and were leading them back to our police car when I heard Detective Bain yell, "Stop or I'll shoot!". We watched as the man who had been driving the truck leaped from the cab and started running.

"Stop or I'll shoot!" Bain repeated. The man kept running. The sound of a gunshot echoed through the morning air. The fleeing man fell.

"Oh Christ!" I thought. "He's shot him." Carl quickly placed our two prisoners in the back of the police car. I watched as Bain and Robinson approached the figure lying on the ground.

"I give up!" the man yelled as the two detectives approached him. The man got to his feet, hands in the air. He was handcuffed and led back to Robinson and Bain's police car.

"Thank God!" I whispered aloud. "They didn't shoot him."

With our prisoners safely secured in the police cars, we called for two uniform officers in a patrol car to guard the truck with its load of meat and the Lincoln until we could have them moved to the police garage. We took Murphy and his two passengers back to police headquarters, placing them in separate interview rooms. On speaking with our prisoners, we learned that Harry's two friends were Richard Brinkman, Harry's brother-in-law and Jimmy Murphy, Harry's brother. Harry refused to implicate either, saying they were just helping him and didn't know the truck and its contents were stolen.

"Look," Harry said. "You've got me. What else do you want?"

We charged all three with shop breaking and possession of stolen property. At their court appearance, they were released on bail. Unknown to Carl or me, the RCMP drug squad, in coordination with our own drug team, had a special interest in Harry Murphy. Several weeks after being released on our charge, Murphy was arrested by the RCMP and charged with possession of heroin for the purpose of trafficking. He was later sentenced to eleven years for trafficking, shop breaking, and possession of stolen property. The charges against Brinkman and Jim Murphy were withdrawn.

Harry Murphy was moved to different penitentiaries over the next several years. In 1974 he escaped, but was quickly apprehended. He was transferred in 1976 to Matsqui, a British Columbia penitentiary. After establishing himself as a trusted prisoner, Harry was called into the supervisor's office one day.

"Murphy", the supervisor said. "We're going to give you one more break. We're going to let you work on trailers, an unsupervised position for trustees." Harry would now work out side the prison confines without a guard.

"One more break," Murphy thought. "That's what I need. One more break."

Murphy took the 'one more break'. It occurred early one morning, while he was working in the unsupervised area. Murphy, unnoticed, walked away from the camp. He made his way to Sparwood, a small British Columbia town and registered in the local hotel using the name Kenneth William Charles Smith. It didn't take Harry long to notice that the night clerk handled a great deal of money. He quickly formulated a plan to 'relieve' the hotel from all that excess cash. Murphy left the hotel early one evening. He stole a car, a shotgun, and a ski mask. Returning to the hotel, he watched from outside until he saw the clerk opening the safe.

As the clerk was about to place the money inside, Harry walked in, aiming a shotgun. He had a ski mask securely pulled down over his face. The terrified clerk handed over the cash. Harry turned and ran from the hotel. He jumped into the car and turned the key. The car wouldn't start. Cursing, he grabbed the gun and the moneybag and dashed from the car. He stood in the parking lot, a shotgun in one hand, the money in the other and the ski mask still covering his face.

"Shit" he said. "What do I do now?"

As he pondered his fate, knowing the RCMP would be on their way to the scene, a car pulled into the lot. Inside were a young man and a woman who were going to register in the hotel for the night. Seeing his opportunity, Harry approached the car, brandishing his gun he ordered the young couple to drive him from the scene. Harry Murphy was now wanted for escaping lawful custody, armed robbery and kidnapping. The robbery and kidnapping charges carried maximum sentences of life. The threesome left Sparwood, driving west through British Columbia, staying at motels along the way.

On the third day, they turned and drove east, returning to Cranbrook. By this time they had formed a friendly relationship.

This is often known as the "Stockholm Syndrome", a condition that kidnapped persons acquire. The Stockholm syndrome was so named as a result of a hostage-taking incident in Stockholm, Sweden. In that incident, a number of 'would-be' bank robbers took bank employees hostage during a botched robbery attempt. They then had a stand off with the police for over a week. During this time the hostages formed a bond between themselves and their captors. When the siege was over, many of the hostages refused to testify against their captors.

Harry and the young couple entered a Cranbrook bar. Inside they met a relative of the girl and some of his friends. After they left the bar, Harry gave the young couple $800.00 for their trouble. They parted company with Harry going his way and young couple driving away in their car. Shortly after, Harry's luck ran out. While touring Vancouver, he was arrested by the Vancouver City Police. Murphy was charged with robbery and kidnapping.

During the trial, the young man who'd been kidnapped testified how he and his girl friend had been taken at gunpoint from the parking lot. He went on to explain how they were forced to drive Murphy to several British Columbia locations before being released in Cranbrook after Murphy took their car. Murphy, who had been slumped over in the prisoners box, jerked up. He leaned over to his lawyer and requested a recess. The judge adjourned court for half an hour. Harry and his lawyer went into an interview room.

"Look," Murphy said, "I didn't steal their car. When I left them, I gave them $800.00 for their trouble. That guy's lying." Murphy's lawyer mused over the strange turn of events.

"Are you telling me the truth Harry?" the lawyer asked.

"Look," Harry continued, "we met a relative of the girl's in a bar in Cranbrook. We sat and enjoyed an evening of drinking with no attempt on their part to escape or tell him they were being held against their will. They had lots of opportunity to escape and didn't do it! I think the weak link is the girl. Give her a shot!" Harry demanded. "I'm looking at big time!"

"Okay let's give it a try." his lawyer sighed.

When the court reconvened, the girl was called to the stand. She also testified as to how Murphy had kidnapped them at gunpoint forcing them to drive to various locations. She said Murphy had stolen their car in Cranbrook. The lawyer questioned the girl relentlessly.

"After you entered the bar in Cranbrook and met your relative, did you tell him you had been kidnapped?" the lawyer questioned.

"No I didn't." she replied quietly.

"Why not?" The lawyer shot back.

"I don't know." The girl replied tearfully.

"Did Mr. Murphy give you some money when he left you in Cranbrook?"

"Yes." came the tearful reply.

"Did Mr. Murphy steal your car in Cranbrook?" the lawyer shouted.

"No he didn't." she replied holding a hand over her mouth.

"What happened to your car after you left Mr. Murphy?"

"We sold it to a car dealer." the witness admitted.

"Are you now telling the court that you lied when you said Mr. Murphy stole your car?"

"Yes." Her reply was barely audible. At this point, the Judge looked sternly at the prosecutor.

"I think we better call another recess until this matter is cleared up." he said.

The Judge then walked briskly from the Court. During the recess, Murphy, his Lawyer and the Crown Prosecutor met. The Prosecutor had been caught off guard. He had no way of knowing his witnesses were lying. Murphy conferred with his lawyer. He knew he had to make a deal that would not be appealed. Murphy's lawyer turned to the prosecutor.

"My client will plead guilty to one count of unlawful confinement," he said sternly, "nothing more, provided he is guaranteed a sentence not to exceed two years."

"I can't accept that" the prosecutor said. "If he pleads guilty to the robbery, we'll drop the kidnapping charge and ask for two years."

"No way!" Murphy broke in. "The Crown could appeal the sentence. It's our way or nothing."

Murphy knew the Crown had lost the credibility of the two witnesses. After further consideration, the prosecutor and defense agreed that Murphy would plead guilty to unlawful confinement of the girl but nothing else. The sentence he received would run concurrent with any time he was already serving. This meant that Murphy would not spend any additional time in jail.

Returning to the courtroom, Murphy pleaded guilty as agreed. He received a two-year concurrent sentence and was returned to Matsqui to face the escaping charge. He received an additional two years. The escaping sentence would be served after his original eleven-year term had been served. He was still eligible for parole. The police never found the money from the robbery Harry said he did. Murphy was sent to Edmonton maximum-security prison. He was released on day parole in 1978. Day parole allows a prisoner to leave the institute during the day to seek employment or to work. He must return at night. Murphy was granted full parole several months later.

A few weeks later as I stepped out of my car in front of my home, I heard someone call my name.

"Bruce, how the hell are ya?"

I turned and looked across the street. It was Harry Murphy.

"What the hell are you doing out of jail?" I asked half jokingly.

"They gave me time off for good behavior." he laughed.

I found Harry Murphy to be a soft-spoken, quiet man; his voice never overbearing or rising to the intensity that often led him into violent confrontation. However, one such incident did occur in June of 1970 and it nearly cost Harry his life. Harry and his friends were eying a local camera shop late one night with the intention of breaking in. They had brought their lady friends with them to avoid police detection. Criminals feel if a woman is in the car, the police are less likely to check them. Murphy and his friends left the girls in the car while they circled the camera shop looking for a vulnerable entrance. While they were gone, a Volkswagen passed the car the girls were sitting in. The driver of the Volkswagen stopped and made a remark to the girls. There was an exchange of words and the Volkswagen drove off. Harry, on hearing the argument, returned to his car and spoke with the girls.

Sitting in the car, he heard the Volkswagen approaching again. He slid down in the front seat. The Volkswagen pulled up along side Harry's car. Again, the driver spoke to the girls. They told him to get lost. The driver of the Volkswagen made some rude remarks. Harry lifted himself from the front seat and challenged the driver. The man drove across the street, parked his Volkswagen, and got out. He stood outside his car as Murphy left his auto and approached the antagonist.

"I'm going to knock your brains out!" Harry screamed at the man.

The driver of the Volkswagen pulled a gun and pointed it at Harry.

"Stay back," he said menacingly, "or I'll shoot!"

"The only way you'll stop me is if you shoot!" Murphy yelled shaking his fist.

The man straightened up, again aiming the gun at Murphy. Harry saw the flame leap from the barrel then he heard the crack. At the same time, he heard a hissing noise coming from his side. He felt no pain. He turned to see if the gunman had hit one of his friends. Everything seemed to stand still. There was an unusual silence as everyone looked on. A patrolling security guard pulled up in his car, looked at the scene, and called the police and ambulance from his car radio. Harry fell to the pavement. As he lay on the road, the water from a street cleaner washed dirt over his face.

"I can't die here." Harry thought. "I can't die in the gutter. What a dirty place to die. I can't die here."

He tried to push himself up from the pavement but slipped into unconsciousness. While Murphy was being rushed to the hospital, his assailant was arrested. The bullet had entered Murphy's left side piercing a lung and collapsing it. The bullet stopped half an inch from his spine, directly behind his heart. Doctors worked desperately to repair the lung. X-rays showed the bullet could not be removed without further endangering Murphy's life. They chose to leave it.

During the trial that followed Murphy's release from the hospital, doctors testified to the severity of the injury. Had the bullet traveled any further, it would have severed his spinal cord. When Harry took the stand, he denied that the gunman had said he was going to kill him. His assailant was found not guilty of attempted murder. Believing that Murphy had lied, the trial judge and prosecutor were not happy. Harry Murphy lived in a criminal element. There is a distorted form of honor among criminals.

At 39, Harry Murphy had faced death several times. None was more bizarre than when he tried to collect an unpaid debt. We knew Murphy lived in a world of violence, often resorting to ruthlessness to accomplish his task. A man with whom Harry dealt, possessed the same characteristics. Among other things, Harry dealt in the lucrative business of drugs when the customers paid. The particular customer elected not to pay for goods received which resulted in a foolish decision that would lead to a violent confrontation. One summer night Harry decided he would drive up to the man's house and pay him a visit. Knowing that the man would have an enforcer, Harry took a baseball bat.

An enforcer is a large intimidating man whose task is to collect bills.

But Harry eliminated the middleman by doing his own enforcing. Murphy entered the small frame house of the drug dealer who had ripped him off.

He noticed the enforcer sleeping on the couch. Attached to his head was a set of headphones. The man didn't hear Harry enter. Murphy raised his bat thinking one 'whack' would do it. The man was a hulk, standing over six feet tall and weighing 250 pounds. Harry didn't want to face the man in hand-to-hand combat. Harry cracked him on the head. The blow wasn't hard enough. In one leap the man was off the couch.

"What the hell's going on!" the man screamed as he stumbled toward Harry.

Murphy lifted the bat again. He whacked him a second time. The man remained firmly on his feet. 'I'm in trouble' Harry thought as the giant, blood streaming from his head made a grab for him. Again, Murphy raised his bat. Again, he brought it down on the head of the enforcer. This time the man turned and ran screaming from the house. Murphy followed him. Again, he hit him. The man fell to the ground. Harry turned and went back into the house. He made his way down the basement stairs entering a bedroom at the bottom. Opening the door, he observed the figure of a man on a cot with a blanket pulled over his head.

"The money I owe you is on the dresser" the man on the cot said.

"I'll get the money later!" Harry said. "I think I owe you a little something for all the trouble you've caused."

In a flash, the man's hand shot out from under the cover, grabbing a gun from a pillow on a nearby chair. The man jumped from the bed and aimed the gun at Harry.

"Out!" he ordered. "Out or I'll blow your fucking head off right here!"

Murphy was not easily intimidated.

"I owe you something", he yelled swinging his bat at the gunman. For the second time Murphy saw flame spit from a gun. He didn't hear the shot, but felt a searing pain in his stomach. He fell to the floor. The gunman stood over Murphy pointing the gun at his head.

"Get up or you're dead." the gunman ordered.

Murphy struggled to his feet. With the gunman behind him, he struggled up the stairs. Murphy staggered through the house and out the door. As he leaned against his car, he asked his passenger to move over behind the wheel and drive him to the hospital. The gunman went back inside.

"I'm okay", Harry said to his friend. "He got me in the stomach, but it's not serious."

Murphy slid into the passenger side as his friend threw the car into reverse. As they backed from the driveway, a police car pulled up behind them. A young Constable approached the car with his gun drawn. When the constable saw that Murphy had been shot, he tried to assist him to the police car.

"He can't wait for the ambulance." his partner yelled.

The pain became unbearable, yet Murphy did not believe it was serious. The ambulance arrived and paramedics administered medical attention to Murphy. He was placed in the ambulance, which rapidly moved back onto the street making its way to the hospital. The enforcer, who by this time had regained consciousness, was taken to hospital in a second ambulance. As the ambulance, carrying Murphy screamed toward the General Hospital, Murphy spoke to the paramedic.

"Take me to the Foothills Hospital" he said.

"Look friend," the paramedic replied, "I don't know if you know it or not, but you're in bad shape. We're taking you to the closest hospital."

Moments later the ambulance pulled into the emergency entrance to the General Hospital. Murphy was rushed into the emergency room. Doctors and nurses rushed to Murphy's side. Intravenous was started. Plasma was administered.

"Take his vitals", a doctor ordered. A nurse strapped on the blood pressure cuff.

"Blood pressure" she yelled "Eighty over zero."

"Something's wrong!" the doctor snapped.

"Try the other arm!" The nurse quickly strapped the cuff on the arm.

"It's the same doctor", the nurse said.

"Impossible" the doctor replied. "He would be dead."

The doctor was right. Harry Murphy was dead. Harry Murphy explained to me what he witnessed in his life after death experience.

"I remember looking down from a corner of the room. I recall this light over my shoulder. I was trying to watch what was happening to me on the table. The doctor was giving me heart massage. The light over my left shoulder kept getting brighter. I had trouble not looking at it. I didn't want to look at the light, but I felt compelled. I wanted to see what was happening to me on the table. The doctor called for the paddles". (These are instruments used to administer electric shock to get the heart beating again.)

"The doctor placed them on my chest. I heard him yell, 'Now!' I saw myself jump as the electricity hit me. My brains were scrambled. I didn't know what was going on. The light over my left shoulder was getting brilliant. I was having trouble keeping my eyes off it. I heard the doctor yell, 'Again'. I knew I didn't want to die. I was scared."

Harry Murphy saw only part of the last heart electrode administered to his body. Twelve days later Harry woke up in his room. He couldn't remember his name. Nurses came in three and four times a day asking Murphy his name. He couldn't remember. It was several days before he did. As Murphy lay in the hospital bed, the incident of the near fatal night kept flashing through his mind. The police attended the hospital wanting to know what happened. Harry told them he couldn't remember. They were frustrated.

On the day of the trial, the doctor who attended to Murphy at the General Hospital testified that the bullet that struck Murphy had fragmented when it entered his body, badly damaging his spleen and liver. His spleen had to be removed. The doctor further testified that Murphy's heart had stopped beating when he was in the emergency room. Clinically, Harry Murphy had died. Only the use of electric shock had restarted his heart.

On the stand, Murphy stated during his evidence that the gun used to shoot him was his. He failed to give other convicting evidence. As a result, his assailant, like the first, was found not guilty of attempted murder. Harry Murphy has since, faced the courts on an assault complaint. He was fined $500.00. While reliving the events of his life, Harry looked at me saying,

"You know Bruce, there's no room out there for a good criminal anymore".

"Well Harry! You can always go on unemployment." I replied.

At the time of writing, Harry Murphy is still an active criminal facing several charges. Both he and I believe that his accusers will testify against him. Because in their minds, as well as the minds of Policeman, "Harry did it".

CHAPTER NINE

No Time to Die

"Unless you quit drinking, you're not going to live to see that young family of yours grow up."

In 1971, the stress I experienced in police work began to manifest itself. This was again, vented by turning to alcohol. Having experienced the problems that alcohol created, I knew what the consequences would be, but I was caught in alcohol's destructive trap. While liquor controlled my life, it also dictated the quality of life to which my family would be exposed. They endured the suffering caused by my violent mood changes, the hunger caused by the channeling of my money to drink rather than food, and the worry of my all night gambling and drinking bouts. I often woke up in places I didn't want to be and with people I didn't want to be with. The end of my shift almost always coincided with my appearance at local drinking spots. Somehow I managed to keep my urge for alcohol under control while on duty. But my off duty imbibing began to affect my job performance. Illness overtook me on a regular basis at work. To avoid my supervisor's suspicions, I remained on duty. Although I managed to hide my problems from my co-workers, I didn't fool my family. Without my knowledge, my wife had sought help from an Alcoholics Anonymous (AA) counselor.

Her action wasn't premature. I was drinking as much as a 26 ounce bottle a day, and often more. Any excuse was used to drink, like making a commendable arrest, losing a court case or being rebuked by supervisors. If I could manage a rationalization, I could manage a drink. Before long, I started to imagine things. I felt my family was against me. Whenever my wife went out, there was no doubt in my mind that she was seeing another man. Trivial and meaningless matters caused me mental agony. If she danced with anyone at a social, or left our table to speak to someone, I would become incensed. Phone calls that my wife received and I didn't understand and her working overtime all led me to believe that it was part of a secret affair she was having. I was tormented beyond description. I turned to the bottle for revenge and self-pity.

A home that had seen happiness and love was filled with fear and suspicion. I was destroying everything that I loved. My children were afraid to talk to me. My wife knew I was driving myself to total destruction. As time passed, I began to have severe stomach pains. When the distress became unbearable, I voluntarily went to the doctor. Dr. Grant Mills, our family doctor, gave me a complete physical examination and made arrangements for me to have my stomach x-rayed. Several days after the tests, I was back in Dr. Mills' office to hear the results.

"The only thing I can find Bruce is a small ulcer," he said. "It can be checked, so there's nothing to worry about. What I am worried about is your drinking," he continued.

"I don't drink that much." I said shifting uncomfortably in my chair.

"That's not what I see," he said sympathetically. "Unless you quit drinking, you're not going to live to see that young family of yours grow up."

I left the doctor's office feeling somewhat relieved. It appeared there wasn't anything seriously wrong with me. But his caution on drinking bothered me. I did have a young family of six children. The twins being the youngest were only eight years old and Gerry, the oldest was seventeen. Although I appeared to be killing myself,

I didn't want to die. I wanted to live to enjoy my family. I immediately quit drinking as suggested by my doctor. When you become addicted to liquor, everything else in your life becomes secondary. Promises you make to yourself and others are broken. You can no longer control the urge for alcohol. Your life becomes unmanageable. Alcohol is cunning, baffling and powerful. My abstinence from it lasted less than a month.

The pains started again. This time they became more frequent and more severe. I started vomiting every day. Once again, I visited Dr. Mills. He sent me to Dr. Bill Novak, a stomach specialist. When I walked into Dr. Novak's office, I felt genuine concern and apprehension. Dr. Novak put me through a series of tests. There was more probing and more discomfort. He gave me an Endoscopy scan. This is a long 'tube-like' scanner that you swallow. A small light attached to the end of the tube scans your stomach. This allows the doctor to probe deep into areas that may be missed on x-rays. Nothing new was found. It appeared as Doctor Mills had said, a small ulcer. The liquor was aggravating the ulcer.

About a week later, while discussing the symptoms with my family, they told me that after consuming large amounts of alcohol, I'd pass out on the couch. Then within an hour I'd be writhing and screaming in pain.

These acts were unconscious to me, so it was hard to believe the stories. Surely I'd have some recollection of such violent seizures. Although the concern on my family's faces had me wondering, I chose to ignore the warning. In an attempt to prevent my drinking, my family played a trick on me one night that should have made me understand the seriousness of my drinking problem. They took a bottle of liquor I'd purchased, poured out the contents and replaced it with plain tea. When I arrived home that evening, I took the bottle from the cupboard and began to drink. As usual, I lapsed into a deep sleep. The next morning I left for work with my usual hangover. On arriving home that night the family told me what they'd done. Their words stunned me. I had become drunk on a bottle of tea.

Experiments done in an American university with drugs show that this will happen to drug addicts. People believing that they are taking drugs will become as high on a placebo as they would on the real thing. It is a psychological reflex. My family in their desperation had tried to show me what was happening. Alcohol was taking over my mind and my body.

I attempted to eat my dinner, putting aside the practical joke, which alarmed me. Once again my dinner was left virtually untouched. I knew that a drink would dispel my fears and put me to sleep, leaving behind the world of pain and anxiety. Upon awakening the next morning, the ever-growing pain gripped my body. I forced myself to go to work. By noon, the shakes had overtaken me. It was impossible to keep my hands from trembling. My partner Carl Gerrard took me to the lunchroom where he ordered me a seltzer. Because I was shaking so badly, as the waitress handed it to me, I spilled it over the counter. Several constables behind me started to laugh. Carl turned in a rage and screamed,

"What's the matter with you assholes! Can't you see this man is sick?"

They looked at each other in amazement. I put the glass down, turned, and walked back to the detective office. That afternoon I went home violently ill. I phoned the doctor and he scheduled me for a series of new tests for the following week.

The tests again, revealed nothing new. Doctor Novak was becoming more concerned. He gave me an antacid to drink saying it would take the gas away from my system that caused the pain. I drank antacid until I though it would kill me, which it almost did. Many times after taking the antacid I would vomit violently, wrenching in pain. The attacks left me completely drained of all strength. My unpredictable moods at home increased.

After bouts of drinking, I'd insist that my wife stay up with me at night. When she refused, I'd go into a fit of rage, knocking pictures from the wall and screaming obscenities. The children lay in their beds terrified. Many mornings when my wife went to work, I'd follow her, convinced that she was meeting someone on the way. The meetings didn't take place, so I'd approach her as she was about to go into the dry cleaning shop where she worked. I demanded to search her purse, believing I would find a phone number or evidence of a meeting place where she was going to meet her lover. After rummaging through the purse and finding nothing to give me cause for doubt, I'd throw it back at her, get into the car and drive home. Back home again, I'd collapse on the couch crying uncontrollably. I felt persecuted, suspicious and I distrusted everyone. I lived in a world of fear. Only sleep or drink would release me from my terrifying world.

One night in December of 1973, my wife begged me not to go to work.

"You look terrible!" she said.

I felt as bad. But I was trying to convince myself that all I had to do was cut down on my drinking and I'd be all right. If I could meet it head on I thought, with a little will power, I could conquer my problem. That night Inspector Hetherington, a long time friend and officer, came into the detective office. For a moment, he studied me.

"You better go home young fella," he said. "You don't look well."

"I'm alright," I snapped.

"Okay boy! But right now you look like you're going to die."

Since my partner was on holidays, I was working by myself that shift. I left the detective office, booked out a detective car and drove around the city. During the evening, I became violently ill, vomiting several times. It seemed now I was beginning to completely understand that I was a very, very sick man. I was sick and flooded with fear of an impending dreadful fate. After learning what had happened the night before, Doctor Novak took me back into the office the next day. Again, he made arrangements for me to go for more tests. Again, he found nothing except a small ulcer.

I had started to lose weight at a drastic rate. My days and nights continued to be filled with drinking, violent mood changes, throwing up and unbearable pain. My wife and I had planned a housewarming one night toward the end of October 1973. At about 5:00 p.m. on the night of the party, the nausea began to overtake me again. As the night wore on, the nausea became increasingly worse. Some of the guests became concerned and wondered aloud if I'd seen a doctor. My sister-in-law came over to where I sat. She looked at me for a moment.

"You're afraid you have cancer aren't you?" Her flimsy attempt to psychoanalyze me wasn't well accepted. I became furious. The thought had never crossed my mind. The doctor knew it wasn't cancer. But my continuing suffering was adding to my sensitivity. As the pain increased, I went to bed, slipping into a deep sleep.

For several weeks after, I remained in a state of constant pain. On January 3rd, 1974, after my wife Nina had gone to work, I sat in the front room drinking. After several drinks, the pain started again. This time it was more intense and severe. By the time Nina came home from work, I was in a state of drunkenness that no longer relieved the tormenting pain. Nina immediately called the doctor ordering him to have me put in the hospital. The next day Doctor Novak called. He'd arranged to have me admitted to the hospital that evening.

I entered the hospital January of 1974. Doctors Mills and Novak came into my room the next morning. They ordered more tests. I had realized that I was losing weight, but had no idea how much until the doctors told me. I had lost 30 pounds in a week. The doctors were baffled by this, but knew my condition was serious.

I was put through more x-rays, blood tests and Endoscopy tests, none of which were new to me. Even with the knowledge that I was an alcoholic and the exhaustive tests, they could not determine my illness.

Two weeks after I entered the hospital, Dr. Mills came into my room with another doctor.

"This is Doctor Jackson," he said. He leaned over and touched my shoulder. "We've decided that we're going to have to operate. Doctor Jackson is the surgeon who will perform the operation.

Right now it looks like your gall bladder, but we won't know until we operate."

"The symptom are all there Bruce," Doctor Jackson broke in, "but the x-rays don't indicate that's what it is." His soft English accent was somehow re-assuring and made me feel at ease. Doctor Jackson stood with hands in his smock looking at me.

"If it isn't my gall bladder, promise me you'll do an exploratory. I can't live with the pain any longer." My voice crackled as I forced the words out.

"Don't worry Bruce," he said patting my shoulder. "We'll find out what's wrong with you one way or the other."

I watched them as they left the room talking in low voices. When my wife came to the hospital that night, I told her what the doctors had said.

"I know honey. I spoke to Doctor Novak today." she said sitting on the edge of my bed and holding my hand. "Everything is going to be all right" she smiled.

She appeared more relaxed, which helped decrease my tension and anxiety. What more could I ask for? I had a loving wife and family and three good doctors. I just knew everything would be okay.

On Friday, January 14th, 1974, Doctor Jackson came into my room. We spoke briefly about my operation. I had lost considerably more weight since entering the hospital. Doctor Jackson was concerned. I was now down to 128 pounds. My weight loss was about 50 pounds in two weeks. We both knew they had to operate quickly.

"We're going to operate on Monday." Doctor Jackson said tapping a pencil against the palm of one hand. "The sooner we get inside you, the sooner we'll know what's causing your problem. If it's your bladder, you'll be back in your room in an hour." His words were uncompromising yet compassionate.

"That's great," I said, heaving a deep sigh of relief.

My wife and children came to the hospital that night. As I sat talking to them, my thoughts turned to the grief and anxiety I'd caused them over the past several years. Feelings of remorse seized me. I could only pray that I'd have the opportunity to repay them for the disregard I'd shown toward them.

Sunday night was a tearful evening. I held Nina's hand; secretly afraid that this may be the last time I'd see her and the children. The agonizing fear of losing my life and leaving my family racked my mind. Before they left that night, I hugged them closely unable to hold back the tears that streamed down my face.

"I'll see you tomorrow honey," Nina said reassuringly as she walked slowly from my room.

Later that evening the male nurse came in to shave me for the operation. As I pulled back the blankets, I lifted my bed attire allowing him to shave my stomach. As I lay with my hands crossed under my head I expressed my concern to him.

"If I didn't think you were going to make it, I wouldn't be here," he said moving the cold blade over my body. He eased my anxiety. A friend who had come to the hospital to pick up his wife from work dropped by. As he was leaving he shook my hand.

"Good luck!" he said.

"Good Luck!" Had his wife told him something I didn't know? Foolishly, I let my mind wander again and the fear of dying once again began to haunt me. As a nurse came in to take my temperature, she noticed my anxiety and gave me a tranquilizer. It settled me down and I soon fell asleep.

The next morning I awoke feeling uneasy. As usual, the nurses came in early. It was January 17th. We discussed my operation. It made me feel better. The nurses moved in and out of the room, rustling their starched uniforms with every step. Their presence allayed my fears. At 10:30 a.m. the head nurse came by.

"You'll be going to the operating room shortly. We're going to give you a needle to make you relax." It didn't. As I lay there wondering about my fate, I heard Doctor Jackson's voice.

"You'll be going up to the operating room now Bruce. We'll see you there."

A nurse and two orderlies entered the room and gently transferred me to a mobile bed. I tried to relax but couldn't. I was so scared I could've screamed. They wheeled me out of my room and down the hallway. I watched the lights on the ceiling slip by. There was a gentle bump as the bed was pushed onto the elevator. When the lights above the floor flashed seven, the elevator stopped. There was no turning back. The nurse and orderlies wheeled me into the operating waiting room. It seemed like an eternity as I lay there waiting. For the first time in my life I experienced the feeling of wanting to turn back the hands of time. I had to fight back the tears. The man next to me looked over.

"What are you in for?" he asked.

"Just my gall bladder." I replied hoping I was right. I wiped the wetness from my eyes. Time passed slowly. Finally a nurse came out.

"Mr. Dubbin?"

"Yes" I replied.

"Okay. Here we go. This won't take long." She wheeled me into the operating room where well-illuminated green figures moved efficiently about. Doctor Jackson spoke to me.

"You won't be here long" he assured me. "You'll be back in your room in no time." he said. His eyes were twinkling under his glasses that looked out between his green cap and mask. My taut muscles relaxed and my thoughts became less dreadful. A nurse approached me, holding two needles on a long cord.

"Okay" she said. "We're going to place these in your wrists. When I do I want you to count to ten." I handed her a sweat soaked Kleenex I had been holding.

"You'd better take this," I said.

"Count to ten Mr. Dubbin."

"One . . . two . . . thr...." The next thing I remember was the outline of a face in the distance. A voice seemed to be calling me. The voice got louder.

"Mr. Dubbin, take deep breaths. Everything is all right." It was the nurse who had given me the anesthetic. Her angelic like face was outlined in a swirl of red hair. "Take a deep breath," she repeated. "Move your toes." I tried. I couldn't. She looked concerned. I couldn't breathe or move! Something had gone wrong! I couldn't say or do anything.

"Call the doctor back!" her voice was loud and commanding. "We're losing him! He's dying! He's dying!"

The words didn't frighten me. Although I was alert enough to understand what was happening, I felt peaceful.

"Get the doctor! We're losing him!" she repeated.

My thoughts turned to my wife and children. They'll be all right. I have lots of insurance. I love them. They'll be all right. That was my last thought as I slipped into unconsciousness. I remember looking down from somewhere above the operating table. I was lying on the table. Somehow it didn't seem strange or unusual. I could see the nurses busy over me. I don't recall seeing any doctors. The next thing I saw was myself being wheeled down the hall into a room. A single room. I watched from above as the nurse and two orderlies gently returned me from the mobile bed onto the hospital bed. Everything faded . . .

Awakening the next morning, I looked up and saw my wife and oldest son Gerry standing by the window next to my bed. They were just watching, as though they'd been there for a long time waiting for me to wake up. As I opened my eyes and looked at Nina, she asked,

"How do you feel?"

"Fine" I whispered. Without thinking I added, "I died on the operating table last night." I expected some response, but there was none.

I slipped in and out of consciousness, mumbling incoherently, not knowing when Nina and Gerry left or what else I had said. For several days after the operation, I remembered little. When I awoke on Thursday morning, I wondered about the experience I had had. I remembered it vividly.

"He's dying!" the nurse had said. If I was, it was the most comfortable feeling I'd ever experienced.

There had been a feeling of peace and warmth, not at all like I had thought it would be. There was no fear. Only tranquility. My thoughts had been only of my family. The possibility of not seeing them again had loomed before me, yet I wasn't afraid. Had I really had an out of body experience, or had it been the anesthetic having an effect on my mind? It was difficult for me to comprehend.

On regaining consciousness, however, the realization that I'd followed the entire episode while unconscious convinced me of what was behind the frightening veil of death. It was something other than eternal sleep that awaits us. I'd been in a state of semi-consciousness most of the week following my operation awakening only long enough to think about my experience. Drugs had been administered to me on a regular basis to kill the pain. I thought little about anything as the drugs kept me in a state of euphoria. For a week after my operation, I remained in critical condition, teetering on the brink of death several times.

I later learned the operation had been a major one. When the doctors operated to check my gall bladder, they found it to be in good shape. They then did an exploratory as they'd promised. As they probed into my body, they discovered a large tumor had formed on my pancreas. A tumor that had swollen my pancreas to three times its normal size. My spleen had been infected and it had to be removed. The doctors were certain I had stomach cancer. A biopsy was performed with the tissue being sent to the lab for tests. As I lay unconscious on the operating table for four hours, the anesthetic continued to seep into my body. The word finally came back from the lab. The tissue was not malignant. I was suffering from pancreatitis, a disease that can be as fatal as cancer. The doctors worked feverishly to remove the infected parts. If I lived, the doctors were sure I'd become diabetic. In the mean-time the anesthetic had clogged my lungs, requiring hasty action by the doctors to clear them so I could breath.

As I entered the second week after my operation, things began to get a little better. The doctors weren't totally satisfied with my slow recovery, but were once again unable to find the cause. Because my condition had stabilized somewhat, the doctors decided to let me go home for a day. Near the end of January my son Gerry picked me up at the hospital and drove me home. Though very weak and drowsy from the drugs that had been continually administered to me, I was thankful to be home with my family.

Most of my day was spent lying on the couch with my thirteen-year-old son Michael constantly at my side. When I left the couch to go to the bathroom, Mike sat outside the door until I emerged, making sure I was all right. We had formed a special bond between father and son. Because of that bond, Mike waited.

Our bond had developed because of our close association with hockey. For seven years I'd coached him. We'd spent many happy hours together. On my return to the hospital later that day, the family accompanied me. Again we experienced a tearful separation. On the evening of January 28th, two days after returning to the hospital, two nurses entered my room with an oxygen tank and mask. As one nurse sat me up, placing the mask to my face, the other lifted my bed gown and began rubbing my back briskly, at the same time telling me to cough. They told me that fluid had gathered in my lungs and had to be cleared out. As I coughed, the pain in my chest felt like someone driving hot knives into my body. I was coughing and choking at the same time. I didn't understand what was happening. During one of my many trips to the x-ray department fluid build up around my heart and lungs had been detected. Nina and Gerry came into the room during the session. I started to cry, asking Nina what was happening. She did not understand either. One of the nurses explained to her that they were trying to clear my lungs of fluid build up. They were very curt telling her if she wanted to know more she would have to contact our doctor. Their concern at the moment had to be clearing my lungs. We couldn't appreciate their attitude at the time. Nina leaned over, telling me they had to go.

"I'll see you tomorrow" she said.

Nina and Gerry left while the nurses kept the oxygen mask on my face. After what seemed like hours, they stopped. They smiled at me, saying they'd gotten most of the fluid from my lungs and that my doctor would see me in the morning. I didn't know that I was once again staring death in the face. The next morning Doctors Jackson and Mills came into my room. They looked concerned.

"Bruce," Doctor Jackson said, "we're going to have to operate again." I stiffened up. I didn't reply. "We have a build up of poison around your heart. We have to operate immediately drain the poison before it does any more damage." Doctor Jackson indicated with his hand the area that the poison was building up in. He stood up, moving away from the bed. "We've scheduled the operation for tomorrow."

Fear seized me again. I moved uncomfortably in my bed, unconsciously straightening the covers, head down. 'I was not getting better' I thought. Once again I would go through the agonizing wait of another operation. What then? Would there be something else? I felt discouraged, as things seemed hopeless. Doctor Mills broke my thoughts.

"Look Bruce! We've got to operate. The poison is building up so rapidly we have to get it drained right away!" It was more of an order than a statement. "It's a delicate operation, but not a complicated one." he went on. "It shouldn't take more than an hour. We have to go through your back and insert tubes under your heart. That way we'll get the poison."

'An hour', I thought. 'Where in the hell have I heard that before?' I lifted my head fighting back the tears.

"I'll do it! But I want your assurance you'll stay in the operating room until I come out of the anesthetic" I said, my voice breaking.

"No problem Bruce. I'll be there right beside you." Doctor Mills replied.

He seemed relieved. I signed the waiver and Doctor Mills and Doctor Jackson left. Again the fears of the operating room raced through my mind. I lay back on the bed with my eyes closed. The anxieties and doubts that plagued me before had returned. The thoughts of my drinking days returned. How could I let this happen? I asked that question many times in the seven weeks I spent recuperating in the hospital. I never found an answer.

January 30th was the day of the operation. The ritual of the needle before going to the operating room; the anesthetist standing by, ready to inject the fluid which would put me into a deep peaceful sleep; the counting before I went under. When I awoke I was lying on my side. The first face I saw was that of Doctor Mills. He was pleased.

"Good work Bruce," he said. "You're doing great!"

I fell back into a deep sleep. I awoke in the room. It was near noon. Several tubes were coming out of parts of my body including my nose, my mouth, and my back. Two days later Doctor Jackson came into my room. After examining my incision, he assured me the operation had been a complete success. The fluids around my heart were draining well. Wednesday morning the nurses removed all the tubes except the one in my back.

I was allowed to sit up in bed. As I sat watching the fluids drain from my body, the realization of what the doctors had said hit home. The massive fluid build up most certainly would have been fatal. After passing my first full month in the hospital, I started to become impatient at my long stay. I questioned Doctor Mills as to how long I'd be in the hospital.

"It took longer than a month to get you here," he said, "don't be impatient. You're doing fine."

I felt like a child being scolded for trying to leave school early. Occasionally I sat up in bed, watching the snow float to the ground or swirl around the window. As allowed, I'd leave my bed, disconnecting the cords that were attached to my back and sit by the window. Outside, the bitterly cold February weather had gripped the prairies. At times, blizzard conditions snuffed out the beauty of the distant Rocky Mountains just as death had attempted to do with my life. Often I could see hospital staff desperately coaxing their coughing cars to spring to life. In the end, the flashing yellow lights of a tow truck answered the call to re-energize the snow-covered heaps of frozen metal. How those lights reminded me of the doctors and nurses whom I watched as they struggled successfully to maintain my spark of life.

Due to the bitter cold, my family at times was unable to visit. But I was content to lie under the warm blankets and pass the time counting my blessings and bask in the satisfaction that I didn't have to venture outside. As before, I was kept well sedated. I had little concern for what was going on around me. Although visitors were present, I often slept, sometimes never remembering who'd been to see me. I felt relaxed and spent so little time in reality that I had no time to worry. Without explanation, oxygen was brought back into my room. I was not concerned and no explanation was offered. I was occasionally given spurts of oxygen. I felt all right and assumed it was part of my recovery, not attaching too much importance to it. The oxygen remained, and I was confined to bed. Late one night, several days later, I woke up to find a nurse standing over me. She was holding my wrist. As I awoke she placed a thermometer under my tongue, taking my pulse at the same time. She withdrew the thermometer and held it up to the light.

"Thank God" she whispered. "It's broken."

"What's broken?" I murmured.

"Your temperature." she smiled. "We were getting a little worried.

I later learned that I'd contacted pneumonia. Once again I defeated the odds. During the middle of February 1974, the tubes were removed from my back. The poison had been drained. I was on my way to what was to be described as a miraculous recovery. One day as Doctor Jackson was examining me, I asked him about my experience on the operating table.

"Doctor Jackson" I said. "What happened to me on the operating table? I died didn't I?" He never looked up.

"You gave us quite a scare. You quit breathing on us. We lost you for a few minutes." He cut the conversation short. I was left wondering when he said, "We lost you for a few minutes." Would I ever know for sure?

Several months later I took in a movie that was based on medical reports of people being declared clinically dead, only to be brought back to life. Their experiences, like mine, took them into a third dimension. A dimension that allowed them to witness themselves being brought back from the unexplained world of death. I paid particular attention to one scene that depicted a woman dying in the hospital. As she left her body, her spirit looked down from a corner of the hospital room that she was in. Then it suddenly occurred to me that the woman was also in a private room as I was when I had my experience. When I left my room for the first operation, I was in a ward with three other patients. When I awoke the next morning, I was in a private room. It was not a surprise to me as I witnessed my movement to the room. Yet being asleep, I should not have known unless I took the everlasting 'one step beyond'. I left the theater knowing in my heart that what happened to me was real.

My recuperation period was not easy. A nurse from the Victorian Order of Nurses visited me daily to cleanse my incision and replace my bandages. I spent many days in a state of deep depression caused by my withdrawal from the alcohol and the drugs that had been administered to me on a regular basis during my long stay in the hospital. The pain often became unbearable. My moods changed by the hour. Many times I secretly wished for a drink to rid myself of those terrible depressions. Unable to cope with the withdrawal symptoms I returned to the doctor.

"I need something to help me through the pain and depression." I said speaking very definitely.

"We'll put you on a mild pain killer. Something that will see you through your recovery period." he responded.

With that he gave me a prescription for Darvon. For the next eight years Darvon would be my constant companion; my new companion.

My loving wife, sweetheart and the woman who experienced the heartache of my years of alcoholism, inserted the following chapter. She shared the worry of my surgery and hospitalization and the agonizing wait, not knowing whether I'd live or die.

~~~

My husband Bruce was a stranger in our home. He wasn't the loving father of our six children, who used to watch over us and make us feel that everything would be all right no matter what happened. This sick, scared man desperately needed our help. After one terrifying night of his drunkenness and uncontrollable fits of rage, I phoned Doctor Novak the following morning. "Doctor Novak this is Mrs. Dubbin. I want Bruce admitted to the hospital right away. Our family is not prepared to stand around and watch Bruce die before our very eyes." I said crying uncontrollably. "You have to do something right away. We can't live like this any longer."

"I was not aware of the mental abuse Mrs. Dubbin. I will make arrangements to have him admitted as soon as I can." The next day Doctor Novak phoned. "I want Bruce at the hospital before 4:00 p.m. today. We'll do some more tests," he said.

After almost two weeks of tests and what seemed like an eternity, the doctor finally confirmed that they were going to have to operate on Bruce.

"We think it's a gall bladder deficiency," he said, "but we'll have to operate to be sure."

I hung up the phone and wiped the tears from my eyes. I knew in my heart it was something more serious. Bruce's excessive weight loss in such a short time told me to expect the worst. I phoned my mother in Vancouver and explained. "Mom, Bruce is in the hospital for an operation. Can you come to Calgary and stay with us for awhile?" I was crying.

"Of course. I'll be there as soon as I can." she replied. "Don't worry honey. Everything will be all right." My mother arrived two days later. The day of the operation came. The surgery was scheduled for noon and the doctor had said he'd call as soon as Bruce was out of the operating room. I awoke that morning feeling depressed and yet relieved that in a few short hours it would be all over. As I sat drinking my coffee, I couldn't restrain the tears from falling. I got Mom up and asked her to phone me at work if there
~~~

was any news on Bruce. I left for work. The day passed slowly. I tried to think about pleasant things like how Bruce would be when he came home.

Two o'clock came and passed. There had been no word from the hospital. When I hadn't heard by three I called. "This is Mrs. Dubbin. Is my husband out of the operating room yet?" I asked the nurse on the ward.

"No' she replied. "He's still in the O.R."

I knew something was wrong. I hurried home from work at 4:00 o'clock. My mother was making supper as I entered. "Is there any word from the hospital mom?" I asked taking my coat off.

"No I haven't heard a thing dear." she replied wiping her hands on her apron. "Did you phone?"

"I called at 3:00 o'clock, but he was till in the operating room." I said anxiously. At 5:00 o'clock we sat down to dinner. There was still no word from the hospital. We ate our dinner in silence. At about 5:30 the phone rang. I jumped up from the table hurrying to the phone. I wiped tears from my eyes as I answered. It was the surgeon.

"Mrs. Dubbin this is Doctor Jackson." came the deep English accented voice. "Bruce is in the recovery room. The operation is over."

"What happened?" I cried. "What took so long?"

"He's resting comfortably" the doctor assured me. "The operation took a lot longer than we had anticipated."

"Is he going to be all right?" I asked anxiously holding back an impending sob.

"Yes, he's going to be all right, but he's going to be a very sick man for awhile. We found a large tumor on his pancreas." the doctor continued.

"We were afraid of cancer and had to do a biopsy to make sure it wasn't malignant. His pancreas was badly diseased and had infected his spleen. Even though the biopsy came back negative, he will probably become diabetic."

I turned away from the children as the tears silently slid down my face. "Then it wasn't his gall bladder?" I inquired.

"No." he said sighing. "His gall bladder was all right. But if he ever drinks again Mrs. Dubbin, it will be like drinking poison. He's lucky to be alive because of the severity of his drinking. We'll just have to be

understanding and patient with him. But he'll be all right in time" he said confidently.

"Thank God" I sobbed. "Can I come up and see him tonight?"

"No" Doctor Jackson replied. "He'll be under heavy sedation tonight. You can come up first thing in the morning."

I thanked him for calling and turned to the children. "The doctor says daddy is going to be all right," I sobbed. I turned and ran to the bathroom, closed the door, put my head in my hands and cried uncontrollably. Even as I cried, I could hear my mother reassuring the children. I washed my face trying to erase the tearstains. Straightening my make-up, I returned to the table.

"Can we go up the hospital tonight and see dad?" Gerry asked.

"No not tonight son" I replied. "The Doctor said daddy will be sleeping. We can go up in the morning." I went to bed that night and softly cried myself to sleep. It was over. Thank God it was over.

The next morning Gerry, my oldest son drove me to the hospital. Bruce had been put in a private room. As we entered, I saw Bruce lying motionless, tubes extending from his body. He looked very sick. I bent over and held his hand as I gave him a soft kiss. Then I stood and waited. Several minutes later, Bruce's eyes opened. He looked over and smiled.

"I died on the operating table last night" he whispered. His voice was deep and hoarse. I didn't respond. He looked like he was in a lot of pain. He kept drifting back to sleep and waking up, mumbling things I didn't understand. Gerry and I stayed for about half an hour. As we were leaving, I leaned over and kissed Bruce. He was asleep. "I love you very much honey and I'll be back to see you tonight." I went home and cried my heart out. I was thankful that Bruce was alive but worried about what the future held in store.

I busied myself fixing up the house and buying new furniture. The kids and I wanted the house to be real nice for daddy when he came home. After surgery, we all expected Bruce to bounce right back. Such was not the case as the doctor warned. After a week Bruce was still very sick and not responding like we thought he would. One evening Gerry and I went to the hospital for our regular visit. When we got to Bruce's room, I saw a sign on the door. OXYGEN IN USE! I was in a panic. We walked into the room and I saw two nurses standing over Bruce. One was rubbing his back and the other was trying to get him to cough.

"What's the matter?" I asked. "What's wrong with him?"

"He's contacted an infection in his lungs." The nurse answered crisply. "If you want to know any more you'll have to contact the doctor."

Bruce was crying. After staying as long as we could, I bent over and spoke to Bruce. We have to go now honey," I said. "We'll see you tomorrow."

"What's happening? Why am I so sick?" he seemed to be pleading for an answer.

"You'll be okay honey, I'll phone the doctor when I get home."

Unable to contact Doctor Jackson, I phoned the resident doctor asking him what was the matter with Bruce.

"He's contacted pneumonia," he said. "He's had a build up of poison around his heart and lungs. We're going to have to operate again to save his life. We'll have to insert tubes behind his heart to drain the poison."

"Oh my God." I thought. How much more can he take? "Will you go and see him?" I pleaded. "He's very scared and doesn't know what's going on."

"I'll slip in and see him tonight." he assured me. The second operation was a success, though the recovery period was long and drawn out. After nearly two months of being hospitalized, Bruce came home. It would be a long time before he completely recovered from his near fatal bout with alcohol.

~~~

Nina and the children suffered severe mental strain, both during my drinking and later when I was hospitalized. The operation and the recovery period all took their toll. For several months after my release from the hospital, we went to family counseling. Each child and Nina and I would tell our stories so we could understand how the other one felt. Denise, our youngest daughter, had been suffering re-occurring nightmares caused by my violent mood changes.
~~~

Almost two months after entering the hospital, I was released. It was a clear, cold day in February 1974 when my son Gerry picked me up and drove me home. Home to my loving family. As we drove through the snow-covered streets, I swore to myself that I'd never again allow myself or my family to suffer the indignities of alcoholism. I'd never again put them through the heartache and pain they'd suffered over the last several years. I'd thank God each and every day for blessing me with health and a beautiful family. I'd never drink again. During my recuperation period, the doctor told me that I wouldn't be a diabetic as they initially suspected. "It's unbelievable," he said. I returned to work in late August of 1974 and was assigned to office duties for a number of months while continuing my recuperation. The doctors who fought so many rounds to save my life have gone now. Death claimed Doctor Mills. Doctors Jackson and Novak moved their practices to other areas.

CHAPTER TEN

On The Lighter Side

It is said a Policemen's lot is not a happy one. However, Policemen must learn to accept situations, occasionally putting a different slant on them. Though we mean no disrespect, we sometimes categorize it as 'Black Humor'. The following stories are a few examples.

'RIGOR MORTIS'

Detective Gaskarth and myself, who had been partners for a year and a half, were split up in 1971 where Gaskarth was assigned to homicide, a unique unit investigating murders and sudden and suspicious deaths. He was partnered with Bob Hay, a homicide detective.

On a quiet fall evening in 1972, Hay and Gaskarth were dispatched to a small apartment building in downtown Calgary.

Reports of a body being found in a 4th Floor apartment had to be investigated.

As Gaskarth and Hay proceeded to the fourth floor, they wondered aloud if they would encounter a murder scene or death from natural causes.

The two Detectives were met in the 4th Floor hallway, by a young man who was clearly distraught. Shown into the apartment, Gaskarth and Hay observed the body of a male victim lying on the living room floor, with his legs together and arms outstretched, looking very much like the famous statue of Christ the Redeemer, displayed on the Corcovado mountain in Rio De Janeiro. Soon, Hay and Gaskarth were joined by Paramedics, who were sent to retrieve the body and transport it to the hospital.

After the detectives completed their initial investigation, the paramedics were advised they could move the body. However, as they attempted to place the body on the stretcher, it became obvious the position of the arms would not allow them to get the body through the doorway of the apartment and onto the elevator.

What to do?

The Detectives decided they would have to manually carry the body to the elevator, then, twist and turn until they could wedge the body onto the elevator.

Once inside the elevator, the two detectives stood the body up against the back of the elevator, arms stretched out, with Detective Hay standing behind the body holding it in place with the frozen arms of the deceased positioned around his shoulder.

The three started their decent to the main floor, however, before they had reached their destination, the elevator stopped on the 2nd floor. As the doors opened, there stood a young girl, probably in her early twenties, hoping to continue down to the main floor. Her eyes widened as she observed the situation inside the elevator.

"Jesus Christ" she screamed as she backed away from the door.

"No!" Hay exclaimed with a straight face. "Its Dr. Abercrombie from the 4th floor."

The elevator door closed and the three continued their journey to the main floor.

Once they arrived at headquarters, the detectives learned the victim, a recently graduated doctor from the United States, had overdosed on prescription medication (pills) and died. He apparently lay on the floor, feet together and arms spread out where he succumbed to the drugs.

'THE BALL'

As a young Policeman in the mid 50's, I had heard many stories of the fabled 'Policeman's Ball'.

Finally, in the early 60's my wife Nina, and I could finally afford to attend the prestigious dance. It was held in the magnificent Palliser Hotel.

As we entered the hotel, and made our way to the Crystal Ball Room, the splendor of the occasion hit. The room was decorated with a dozen crystal chandeliers and attended by men and women in smart black tuxedos with starched white shirts who greeted us as we entered the room

Senior officers in their dress uniforms stood in small groups chatting and laughing.

My wife and I made our way to our table, where we soon became engaged in conversation with other young Police Officers. Soon our attention was drawn to the ballroom entrance as a Senior Constable entered the room accompanied by his date, a 'drop dead' gorgeous woman.

As they made their way across the ballroom floor to their seats, the conversation at our table acknowledged she was a beauty. The 'belle of the ball'.

Later in the evening, while visiting the men's washroom, I engaged in conversation with a Sergeant, known as a braggart. He immediately bragged about the fact he was familiar with the Constable's gorgeous date. 'I've had her more than once', he bragged while standing over a urinal ridding himself of the liquor he had consumed. 'Ya' he repeated. 'I've had her more than once', he bragged as he dried his hands, left the washroom and returned to his table. I returned to my table explaining to the others what the Sergeant had said. 'I don't believe it', a constable stated. 'She's too classy for him.'

What a glorious night it was as my wife and I danced the night away on one of the most entertaining nights we had had in our nine plus years of marriage.

Several weeks later while entering the parade room for duty, I heard a voice. 'Hey Dubbin', a Constable called. 'You know that chick the Sergeant bragged about 'doing' several times? She was arrested last night'.

'It appears that she, is a he; a cross dresser; a male prostitute', he laughed. 'Ask the Sergeant about ALL those times he had her'. I did not!

'THE PURSE AND THE PUG'

In the early '70's, Bill Gaskarth and I were both promoted tot the rank of detective. We were assigned to G.I.S. general investigation squad. In 1971, we were partnered. One of our first assignments was patrolling the South West part of the city.

On a sunny afternoon in September, we were called to an address in Roxboro, a quiet community. We expected it to be a routine call. It did not turn out that way.

Pulling up in front of the address, a well kept bungalow, we approached and rang the door bell. The door was opened by a stately looking woman in her mid 60's. She invited us into the living room asking us to sit on a sofa. The complainant sat directly across from us.

When questioned about the housebreaking, she stated she had had a party the night before.

While partying in the lower family room, someone had entered an open rear door and stole her purse and contents.

As she was talking, a small pug nosed dog entered the room. The complainant bent down, and picked the dog up and placed it on her knee facing us.

The dog, a wall-eyed pet, had its tongue hanging out the side of it's mouth and was panting heavily. It was the ugliest dog I'd ever seen.

The complainant continued, her story telling us the purse had fifty dollars and personal items in it. As she spoke, the dogs penis slowly emerged from it's sheath. Bill and I locked at each other barely able to control our laughter. The penis then retreated to its sheath.

The complainant was not privy to this view.

Detective Gaskarth and I continued to take notes.

The complainant continued describing the contents of the purse, reiterating that it contained fifty dollars. On cue, the dog's penis once again shot from its sheath.

Unable to contain my laughter, I stood up and excused myself, saying I was going to check the yard for the purse.

The complainant gave me a sideways glance as I left the room.

Detective Gaskarth was left attempting to stifle his laughter while I retreated to the front yard rocked with laughter.

As the complainant continued, in an attempt to avoid the dog's antics, Gaskarth turned and looked out the front window only to see me leaning against a tree, shoulders rocked with laughter.

Bill lost it and burst out laughing. He also excused himself from the complainant saying he would go out and help me search for the purse. The complainant, believing we were laughing at her plight, complained to the duty inspector about the rude way we had handled her complaint.

Once we had explained our side to the inspector, he was more understanding than the complainant.

'THE RABBIT'

During the fall of 1967, Detective Boyd Davidson, Detective Dick Houger and myself, a constable at the time, attended a murder trial in Toronto.

While working the front counter in Calgary, I had arrested a housebreaking suspect by the name of Dennis Dale Robertson, recently of Toronto. Robertson was later interviewed by Davidson and Houger and held for a Toronto murder. (By Judge Alone)

I had expressed some concern to Detective sergeant Bob Pittman after the arrest, suggesting Robertson had more on his mind than a housebreaking.

Arriving in Toronto, we checked into our hotel and met with the Toronto homicide unit. After being introduced to other Toronto detectives, we were shown the Toronto night-life and were treated like royalty. Toronto had the most successful homicide unit in Canada. We soon learned Toronto would not be a city one would want to commit a crime. You did so at your own peril.

Two of the more 'colorful' detectives we met were known as "Lumpy and Shakey", two detective whose nicknames they acquired over the years. They worked robbery detail and had quite the reputation. Hearing several of their stories convinced us they had certainly earned their reputation.

Several years before our arrival, the two had arrested a bank robbery suspect.

Taken to headquarters the suspect was placed in an interview room where Lumpy and Shakey began their interrogation with the usual question. Name? Address? Do you have a record? Have you ever been arrested? The suspect answered candidly.

"Ever robbed any banks?" he was asked.

"No!" came the reply. "Never?"

Lumpy repeated sarcastically. "No!"

"I don't rob banks!" the suspect replied,

"Really!" Shakey shot back. "We don't have time to piss around with you all day. We're going for a coffee. Think about it!" they yelled as they exited the room.

While the suspect was pondering his fate, the interview room door opened. The suspect sat stunned as a six-foot tall rabbit with a three foot carrot entered. Without a word, the rabbit raised the carrot and started beating the suspect around the arms and shoulders.

"What the fuck are you doing?" screamed the suspect as he attempted to protect himself from the blows.

Moments later the rabbit left the room without uttering a word.

While the suspect sat shaking in his chair, the door opened and Shakey and Lumpy walked in.

"What do you assholes think you're doing? Sending a rabbit with a carrot to come in her and beat me!" the suspect screamed.

"Don't know what you're talking about." Shakey replied.

"Ya!" Lumpy echoed. "All we're trying to do is solve a few robberies."

"Well I don't know what you're talking about." The suspect repeated.

"We'll give you a few more minutes to think about it," the detectives said as they left for the second time.

On cue, the door opened and in walked the rabbit. Again, without a word, the bunny lifted the carrot and began to beat the suspect harder and more rapidly.

"Leave me alone!" the suspect screamed.

The rabbit continued to beat the suspect ignoring his pleas. Then once again, without a word, the rabbit turned and left the room.

As Lumpy and Shakey re-entered the room the suspect screamed,

"I'm telling the judge! You send a rabbit in here to beat me with a carrot and you think you can get away with it? Well you can't! I'm telling!" the suspect repeated."

"So you're going to tell the Judge we left and sent a rabbit with a carrot in to beat you?" Shakey asked.

"Go ahead" said Lumpy. "They'll send you to the funny farm so quick you won't know what happened."

"Come on" Shakey said. "We're outta here. Who know's. Maybe the rabbit with the big carrot will come back." They started leaving the interview room.

"Don't go!" the suspect screamed. "I'll tell you what you want to know."

Moments later, the suspect admitted to eight armed robberies. He was booked, and charged. At the trial the suspect pleaded guilty and was sentenced to 10 years.

'THE TRIAL'

While in Toronto on the Roberson trial, I attended several other hearings.

One such case involved the rape and murder of a 12 year old girl. The suspect, a 22 year old man, had been arrested and interrogated by the homicide division. The interrogation lasted for over 20 hours with no sleep or breaks. It was relentless. The suspect broke down and took the investigators to the area where he hid the knife and clothing of the young murder victim.

At the trial, the defense Council objected, vigorously as to how the evidence was obtained.

"The accused was not given the benefit of council nor was he allowed a meal or breaks. This evidence was obtained under duress.", the lawyer argued. "It should not be allowed."

The Judge leaned back, hesitated for a moment then replied,

"I am not concerned as to how the evidence was obtained. My concern is if the suspect told the truth. He obviously did, as he lead the detectives to the victims clothes and the knife. All the evidence is admitted. I find the accused guilty."

'RUN TOM RUN'

After joining the police service in 1955, I walked the beat for several years before being promoted to patrol cars. As I rose through the ranks from rookie to 1st class constable I was assigned to cars which was a much more desirable position.

One night in early February 1968 constable Tom Gorman and I were assigned to a south side unit. Tom, a retired military policeman was a large man, weighing over 200 lbs. He was nicknamed 'Spook' because he often heard and saw things that other Policemen did not.

At about 1:30 a.m. we heard officers calling for assistance as they pursued a car fleeing from a downtown shop breaking. The culprits were heading east toward Scotsman's hill, an area overlooking the Stampede grounds and the Elbow River. The hill was so named because of the hundreds of spectators who lined the hill during Stampede events, including the nightly fireworks. I threw the car into low gear, spinning the wheels and throwing gravel behind us as we took up the pursuit. As we proceeded to the location, patrol units were informed that the culprits had abandoned their vehicle and were on foot running through yards in the area. Gorman spotted the two suspects and jumped from the patrol car screaming as he ran, "they're over here". I slammed the car to a halt and joined Tom in the chase. Tom ran between two houses and disappeared from sight. As I reached the edge of the cliff, I looked over the top and spotted Tom hanging from a bush like an apple from a tree. I quickly removed my winter jacket, and cautiously handed it to Tom, who grabbed on with one hand while I carefully pulled him to safety. Once back on top, our eyes searched the darkened night looking for the culprits. Tom spotted them as they slid down the hill and ran through the deep snow behind the horse barns. We started our descent down the hill trying to keep the suspects in sight. We soon spotted them again, running behind the horse barns and heading for the main tributary of the Elbow River.

Although Tom was a much heavier man than I, he gained on the culprits as I ran behind. Through the Stampede grounds they went, down the banks and onto the ice of the Elbow River. As I reached the river, I could hear the ice cracking while the three continued their race. Although I was a fair distance behind them, I was half way across the river when I felt the ice give away. In an attempt to reach the safety of the south bank I sped up, but suddenly felt the ground collapse from under me as I fell into the icy depths of the Elbow River. I was surprised to find myself standing waist deep in the frigid water and was able to make my way to shore, where I sat shivering on the banks. Within minutes, a patrol car, manned by constable Kevin May, pulled up to the bank and transported me back to headquarters.

Meanwhile, as constable Gorman continued his pursuit up the bank and into Burns cemetery, he fell into an open grave. He later explained to a reporter that, "The minute I felt myself falling, my feet took wings and I was out of that hole in seconds".

Tom continued his pursuit following the suspects to a house on 47 Avenue Southwest where he had a motorist call for assistance. The shop breakers were soon in custody and eventually received 2 years jail time. Tom certainly did not allow anything to 'Spook' him that night.

'A TENDER MOMENT'

Many years after the investigation by Detective Bill Gaskarth, of young Carol Marie Veregen, Bill shared a moment that can now be considered tender and slightly humorous, considering the outcome of Carol's horrific encounter. While interviewing young Carol to obtain details of the vicious attack on her life, Detective Gaskarth gave her a pen and piece of paper to write down the answers to the questions he was asking her because she was not able to talk. As she bravely recounted and wrote the details of the attack, she handed Bill her answers and he promptly began writing out more questions for her on the piece of paper. As he handed his next question to the young victim, she looked at him quizzically and wrote 'Why are YOU writing it out? I can still hear!' He grinned sheepishly, smiled, and turned red as he realized what he had done.

CHAPTER ELEVEN

The Scales of Justice

"...laws are like cobwebs which catch small flies, but let wasps and hornets go free". Jonathan Swift

Criminal offences, once punishable by death in Canada, included stealing turnips. Hanging was the method of execution. This penalty for such a petty crime was provided for under British law prevailing in Canada until 1859. The nature of crimes demanding execution decreased over the next 125 years until, in 1976, Parliament abolished the death penalty. Capital punishment was replaced with life imprisonment without eligibility for parole for 25 years. Also, in 1976, Parliament amended the Criminal Code by adopting Section 745, known as the faint hope clause. Section 745 allows murderers to seek early parole after serving just 15 years of their 25 year sentence. The amendment has, in fact, turned cold-blooded killers into celebrities by giving them media coverage and allowing them to go before the courts to ask that the 'so called' life sentence be reduced from the mandatory 25 years. Such rights not only give killers access to the courts for the revolting purpose of pleading for less time, it also draws national attention to them and their repulsive crimes; attention many seem to enjoy.

Hearings trigger emotional trauma in the victims' families. But the murderer's 'rights' cannot be interfered with. The wife of RCMP Constable Brian King, executed in Saskatoon in 1978 by Gregory Fisher and Darrel Crook, experienced this pain twice when the killers of Constable King appeared in a Saskatoon court to reveal how they had been rehabilitated. They took courses and . . . . found Christ!! More recently, Clifford Olson, better known as the Beast of B.C. who raped, tortured, and then murdered at least 11 children, was flown to Vancouver by private jet and protected like royalty. Relatives of his victims had to make it to Surrey, B.C. on their own, only to see Olson sneer at them from behind bullet proof glass as they gave impact statements.

There have been close to 90 requests for early parole under Section 745 since it was adopted in 1976. In B.C. where Olson's case was reviewed, there have been 9 reviews and 6 recommendations for early release.

In Saskatchewan where the killers of Constable King pleaded their cases, there have been 5 applications heard and 3 recommendations for early release. The entire picture across Canada is no better from the victim's side. Of the 83 cases heard, almost 70% of criminals received early release. Further, the number still eligible to apply is in the hundreds—and this includes Paul Bernardo, a dangerous sex killer.

Canada's criminal justice system, which provides for such disgusting pampering of murderers, consists of a variety of agencies. It extends from lawmakers to all police forces across the country. Sandwiched in between, are courts, lawyers, prosecutors, and the parole board. Spin offs of these are counselors, halfway houses, and private agencies designed to help those on parole.

Municipal and federal police services are those people expected to maintain law and order. Canada's Criminal Code controls both. Lawmakers in Ottawa, who are guided in many ways by decisions that are handed down by the Supreme Court of Canada, prepare the Code. Legal minds spend months, even years carefully defining each section of the Code. Regardless, the Criminal Code is a statute that has been bitterly criticized by most Canadians. They consider that each change gives the criminal, especially murderers, a little more opportunity to remove the prison bars. Section 745 is the most outstanding example. Turnip thieves would have appreciated this consideration in the 1800's. Prior to Section 745 being adopted in 1976, several studies done in the 1960's on detention and sentencing resulted in such legislation as the "Bail Reform Act", "Mandatory Supervision" and of course, the abolishment of capital punishment.

The "Ouimet" report of 1969 suggested that sentencing should not stress revenge but rehabilitation and deterrence. Consistently, new legislation introduced to balance the scales of justice, as was the intention of the Ouimet Report, has done much more for the criminal than the victim. Section 745 of the Criminal Code was adopted to encourage good behavior from those sentenced to life imprisonment, which usually means 25 years.

A relative of one of Clifford Olson's victims drew an analogy between Section 745 and a schoolteacher letting pupils out of school early provided they behaved during the day. "Would it not be more appropriate," the relative asked, "to keep misbehaving children in after school than to reward them for behavior that is reasonably expected of them?" A good question!! The Criminal Code also provides for what is known as a "Day Pass". It is allowed three years before the full parole eligibility date. It has also allowed dangerous criminals back into society for what is supposed to be brief periods to help them "adjust".

Wayne Boden, a serial killer convicted in 1972, rode a "Day Pass" to temporary freedom in 1984. The "Pass" was issued less than a year after he had been refused parole from his life sentence. He had been refused because officials considered he would kill again. Although the Criminal Code makes provisions for "Day Passes", various acts also give criminals special consideration. In 1976, eight years before Boden was allowed to roam Montreal streets, a British Columbia court released two men under the provisions of the "Bail Reform Act". Both men had been charged with murder. Their release resulted in a shoot-out that ended with the death of a Calgary Police Officer. The Bail Reform Act provided another criminal with the opportunity he had been seeking. After being charged with kidnapping and assaulting his ex-girl friend, he was released as provided by the Act.

The offender, Atilla Kenders, promptly kidnapped his girl-friend Karen Sirdar again, murdered her, and then thoughtfully committed suicide. In 1979, a Pass was issued to another criminal. This man, Kristen Kjeldsen, although found innocent by reason of insanity, was given an un-escorted pass from Alberta Oliver Hospital. Of course, Passes are issued to patients for a specific period of time. According to rules, which seem unenforceable, the patient must return at the expiration of the Pass for further treatment. The Pass delivered to Kjeldsen delivered death to another.

If this Act has benefited anyone, it is hard to imagine whom. Several Judges detained a man who raped a woman from a Calgary escort service. A plea to Justice Virgil Moshansky resulted in the man's release. But poetic justice walked hand-in-hand with criminal justice in this case. After raping three more women while enjoying the freedom given to him by Justice Moshansky, the sex offender faced Justice Moshansky again, who had the task of sentencing this rapist. On conviction, the man received 18 years.

It is evident that there has been no balancing of justice as intended by the Ouimet report. As a matter of fact, new legislation adopted as a result of this report has given criminals the opportunity to re-offend, thereby creating more victims, but no fewer criminals. Mandatory supervision is very deceiving. The purpose of the provision was to assure the public that violent, unpredictable criminals would receive close supervision while finishing the last one-third of their sentence.

But in at least one instance, the Wayne Boden case, it was determined that at one point during his Day Pass he was under absolutely no supervision. In another "mandatory supervision" case in 1974, a man described by prison officials as a psychopath was released from prison.

In a deadly confrontation with Calgary Police, he killed one Policeman and wounded eight. It seems evident that "Day Passes",

"Mandatory Supervision", the "Bail Reform Act" and Bill 745 were adopted strictly for the criminal. In addition to this, courts, victims, and the general public are bombarded with accusations that the criminals "rights" are being trampled. Here again it seems that the "Canadian Charter of Rights" leans more towards the Criminals than the Victims.

CHAPTER TWELVE

The Justice System

'....we have decided from now on to stress the rehabilitation of individuals rather than protection of society.'

Little has changed over the last 50 years to improve the justice system. Criminals are now given credit for "dead time", which is time spend in custody awaiting trial.

Judges appear to write their own laws, often rendering decisions that do not follow the criminal code guidelines.

A Doctor in Quebec, who admitted killing his two young children, was found not guilty by a Quebec judge.

An Alberta judge found two young offenders not guilty of murdering an elderly couple.

The two youths were arrested and were in possession of the elderly couple's stolen truck and charged with two counts of murder.

Charges were dismissed when the judge refused to allow certain statements to be admitted.

As of May, 2012, the RCMP have re-charged one of the original offenders with two counts of first degree murder.

Prosecutors are not faultless because often they don't appeal the rulings.

(Goyer Quote) "Some view the correctional system as the mechanism for the infliction of the punishment component of the sentence, but it is clear to the Panel that the 'punishment' and deterrent component of the Criminal Code's sentencing principles is achieved by the incarceration of the individual—the offender goes to a penitentiary as punishment, not for punishment. The correctional system is therefore responsible for implementing the rehabilitation principle as part of its overall mandate to protect public safety, thereby linking CSC to the broader criminal justice system in Canada.

To make it clear, the Panel has taken the position that an individual is sentenced to a penitentiary as punishment. CSC delivers on that principle by admitting the individual to one of its institutions and, within the limitations of the original sentence ordered by the courts, hold that individual until it is determined that he or she can safely be returned to society. CSC then imposes the various restrictions on the offender's personal liberty in order for the correctional system to deliver on the rehabilitation principle.

It was with this intent that legislators in 1992 created the legislative mandate of CSC, which states:

> *The purpose of the federal correctional system is to contribute to the maintenance of a just, peaceful and safe society by: carrying out sentences imposed by courts through the safe and humane custody and supervision of offenders, and assisting the rehabilitation of offenders and their reintegration into the community as law-abiding citizens through the provision of programs in penitentiaries and in the community.*

It is the view of the Panel that this mandate of control and assistance remains as relevant in 2007 as it did in 1992, and will continue to serve the Service and the Canadian public well into the future. However, the Act does not discuss the importance of the balance between CSC's responsibilities and the offender's responsibilities."

One has to wonder what influence the following statement made on the general public.

"Jean Pierre Goyer decreed in 1971, under the leadership of Pierre Elliott Trudeau, Liberal Prime Minister of Canada.

'The longstanding historical debate over crime, punishment, and the correctional system is essentially a discussion of the extent to which punishment overshadows or is overshadowed by efforts to correct criminal behavior. This debate has taken place politically and in academia.

On October 7, 1971, Solicitor General Jean Pierre Goyer announced in the House of Commons, the Government's intention to stress rehabilitation of criminals even though it posed a risk to the public. He went on to say that:

> *...too many Canadians disregard the fact that the correctional process aims at making the offender a useful and law-abiding citizen, and not any more an individual alienated from society and in conflict with it. Consequently, we have decided from now on to stress the rehabilitation of individuals rather than protection of society.'"*

Long before 1971, Canadians suffered the consequences of the courts making irrational decisions on what appeared to be a closed case. An example of such a case occurred in Toronto in October of 1967 (By Judge Alone) when Chief Justice Leif of the Ontario Supreme Court used all kinds of excuses to dismiss evidence that in my opinion was properly obtained, resulting in the dismissal of a murder case. (By Judge Alone).

Hundreds if not thousands of such cases have since been recorded. While our daughters and children are raped and murdered, the courts appear to follow the direction of the Solicitor General.

The Prison reforms are generally molded to ássist those willing to be assisted. Little is done to discourage those who have violent tendencies or who are repeat offenders.

"Oh, what a tangled web we weave, when first we practice to deceive!"

Sir Walter Scott, Marmion, 1808

Epilogue

Bruce Dubbin retired from the Calgary Police Service in 1983, at the age of 51. It was not until 1985 that he took his last drink. There were still struggles in his relationships at home, but in November 1990, lots of things changed. Although he only achieved a grade eight education, Bruce was an excellent student, and had always excelled at studying. He spent months prepping for his real estate exam, and as with every test he took as an adult, he aced it. He wanted to be the best at whatever he did, and in spite of several setbacks early in his career, Bruce worked hard to achieve success in the real estate industry. He worked late nights, and would often go to the office on the weekend to get things done while there was no one else around.

It was a Saturday afternoon, and Bruce was alone at the office in the Northwest of Calgary. He began to feel nauseous, had some numbness in his arms and chest pains. Bruce called his son Mike and asked him to come and pick him up at the office and drive him home. Luckily for everyone, Mike had just finished a first aid/CPR course on the previous weekend, and recognized the symptoms Bruce described as those of a heart attack. Mike hung up the phone and called 911, and gave the operator the location of the office and the symptoms described by Bruce. Paramedics arrived and transported Bruce to Foothills hospital, where it was confirmed that Bruce had suffered a heart attack. Mike was overwhelmed with emotion when the doctor confirmed that had he not done exactly what he had done, Bruce would have died alone in his office.

Bruce survived a pancreatic tumor, three heart attacks, and over the next fifteen years, was a lot more to come. Diabetes, emphysema, ulcerative colitis, and two more heart attacks were in his future. Bruce has survived all of it.

Today at the age of 80, he maintains a full time job in the security industry, and continues to be in touch with his friends (all retired) from the Calgary Police Service. Bruce and Nina remain happily married after fifty nine years. After spending over 30 years working as a police officer, communications officer, and Court and Prisoner officer, Bruce has not changed his opinion on the Canadian Justice system. He feels, as do the majority of Canadians, that too much emphasis is placed on the rights of the accused, and even the convicted, and very little is placed on the rights of society at large to be protected from predators with a record of violent crimes. Watching prisoners such as Clifford Olsen continue to torture his victims from prison through correspondence with the virtual blessing of corrections officials, is mind boggling to all of us. Bruce tries to shed light on this in his book, and I believe his stories highlight the need for drastic change.

Ken Dubbin, Victoria, B.C